Let the Children Lead

Other Books by Nelson Cowan

Worship Any Time or Place

Nelson Cowan

Let the CHILDREN LEAD

Models for Worship with All Generations

Abingdon Press
Nashville

LET THE CHILDREN LEAD:
MODELS FOR WORSHIP WITH ALL GENERATIONS

Copyright © 2025 by Abingdon Press

All rights reserved.

No part of this work may be reproduced or transmitted in any form or by any means, electronic or mechanical, including photocopying and recording, or by any information storage or retrieval system, except as may be expressly permitted by the 1976 Copyright Act, the 1998 Digital Millennium Copyright Act, or in writing from the publisher. Requests for permission should be addressed in writing to Permissions, Abingdon Press, 810 12th Avenue South, Nashville, TN 37203 or emailed to permissions@abingdonpress.com.

ISBN: 9781791039578

Library of Congress Control Number: 2025938840

Scripture quotations unless noted otherwise are from the Common English Bible. Copyright © 2011 by the Common English Bible. All rights reserved. Used by permission. www.CommonEnglishBible.com.

MANUFACTURED IN THE UNITED STATES OF AMERICA

Contents

vii	Introduction
1	Chapter 1: Unlearning and Reframing
13	Chapter 2: Pray-Grounds
25	Chapter 3: Sensory Sensitive Worship
39	Chapter 4: Intergenerational Outreach
53	Chapter 5: Church-School Partnerships
67	Chapter 6: Children in Contemporary Worship
79	Chapter 7: The Old Has Gone, the New Is Here
91	Conclusion: No Longer Strangers or Guests

Introduction

It was 1994, and I was five years old. My parents felt like we should probably go to church, so we chose the United Methodist church down the street from us—the same one I went to for preschool. We had a few Methodists in our family, but that was not an ecclesial banner we waved high.

As a child, I remember the feeling of dread each week, waking up early to get ourselves to the 8:30 a.m. guitar-led contemporary service. Once we got there, we sat near the front on the left side of the red-carpet-adorned sanctuary. We sang some songs. The worship leader was bearded and smiley. I remember the song "Lord, I Lift Your Name on High" being a crowd favorite, and mine too. We heard sermons every week, though I don't remember those. We received Holy Communion at the altar rail monthly—the bread, small and chewy; the juice, sweet. I cherished my role in being the one to leave a few dollars at the rail. For what purpose? No clue.

I was often bored during the non-musical parts of the service. I doodled on the offering envelopes. Sometimes I played quietly with toys from home. Most of the time, I would lie down in the pew, wishing the service would end soon.

After the service was Sunday School. I went a couple times, then refused to go anymore. My parents complied, but probably because they also weren't jibing with their class.

On some Wednesday nights, we attended dinners in the multi-purpose space known as the "Family Life Center." I remember eating spaghetti with

Introduction

meat sauce and garlic bread. I also recall the large special needs ministry with folks who looked, spoke, and acted a bit differently than I was accustomed to.

I have a faint memory of getting a very "supporting" role in the children's musical production. There were costumes involved. My parents were not too happy at just how "supportive" my small role was.

One summer, I attended Vacation Bible School. I'm not sure if I made it through the whole week. I memorized 1 Timothy 4:12 and sang a song about the Egyptian pharaoh accompanied by some snazzy hand motions.

For one or two years in the fall, we helped unload pumpkins from a big truck to stock up the pumpkin patch.

We attended that church on and off for 6 years.

Then, we left that church, never to return as regular worshipers.

Did something go wrong here in the spiritual formation of young Nelson in worship? What about for my parents? Perhaps you may be thinking there was not enough spiritual depth from the senior leadership at the church. Or it could be the Christian education program being not up to snuff. Maybe the music was bad (I mean . . . it was . . . but it was the 90s). Or perhaps we were not given service opportunities or leadership roles quickly enough (well, we had those too).

The truth is that the answer does not always lie within the institution or its leadership. After six years, the church simply never felt like *home* to us.

However, when I look back, this church was *exactly* what I needed. This church was *exactly* what my family needed. Following the wisdom of the scriptures to "train up a child" and Jesus's charge to welcome the children, this church created space for me to be a worshiper.

I do not see this as a failure of the church to retain our family.

But how often do we as pastors and leaders pin that blame on ourselves? It must be something about us, our church, our programming, our *this* or *that*. As a pastor in The United Methodist Church, I've sat in on those speculative meetings before.

"Why did this family leave?"

"We did everything we could to make them feel welcome."

Introduction

"We have a preschool here at the church. Why do none of these families attend on Sunday morning?"

Our biggest failure is not programming or personnel.

It's that we have been conditioned to view the formation of children in worship as a means to an end.

I wish this *end* were something noble, such as the glorification of God, the sanctification of humanity, or the inbreaking reign of God on earth as it is in heaven.

But that's not it.

When it comes to our programming with children, too often we are in the business of *institutional preservation*. The perpetuation of our houses of worship.

Here is a series of phrases. As a pastor or leader, how many of these—or versions like these—have you heard, or perhaps said yourself?

"We need more young families with children because we need a new generation to keep the church going."

"We need to do *something* that will attract children. What new ministry should we start?"

"If we do not have X, Y, Z program(s), the kids won't stick around."

"Children need to be entertained."

"Once we get [this person / this family] plugged into the church, I can finally step down from my leadership role."

Since the mid-twentieth century, polling organizations and news agencies have been sharing about the decline of Mainline Protestantism, and in general, organized religion in the United States. The United Methodist Church, for example, has seen consistent numerical decline in membership since its inception in 1968. For many who were raised in the church—whether in the UMC or in another Mainline denomination—this narrative of decline has been a consistent source of anxiety.

In the minds of many well-intentioned people, getting children involved in worship and Christian education was the silver bullet to combat this decline. The logic went something like this: if the children are involved, they will mature into adulthood and still be connected to the church, get married, have their own children, then replicate the cycle—in that *same church*. Of course, now we can point to why that was not a viable model, whether it's the greater mobility of people, the proliferation of technology that keeps us connected across vast distances, the diversification of the family unit, or the perceived secularization of the religious landscape of the United States.

Many churches now recognize that the children in their current programs will likely not remain in the same congregation as they mature into adulthood. Yet, when incorporating children into worship, we often make programmatic decisions as if the primary goal were institutional preservation. This lingering anxiety helps explain why ministry with children has so often been framed in transactional terms.

Put simply, *a "transactional" model of ministry is when churches or ministries make intentional programmatic changes with the hoped-for outcome of increased attendance, participation, or commitment to the organization.* To be clear, the desire for a positive transaction is not a bad thing. Of course we want incarnational churches that adapt to the needs of communities and are contextually rooted! However, what we often lack is the pastoral imagination to see ministry with children and families in ways beyond the preservation of our institutions.

This book is not about growing your ministry with children with the intended outcome of institutional survival. I will not be offering quick tips to enhance your church programming and grow your congregational membership tenfold. Instead, I am interested in crafting more faithful approaches that reframe our transactional thinking about engaging children in worship.

This is a book about models of worship with children that you can learn from to enhance your own ministries. It rests on the fundamental claim that children are worshipers in their own right, worthy of respect, trustworthy of agency, and are best served by worship practices with all generations present. It is written to pastors and leaders in local congregations looking to serve the youngest disciples in faithful and authentic ways.

After some theological grounding in chapter 1, chapters 2 through 6 offer five different models of congregations who are doing faithful work

Introduction

in empowering children in worship. I want to highlight their stories of success and for us to glean their wisdom. Importantly, these congregations vary in membership size; they have different breakdowns in age, race, and class; they are geographically diverse; and they run the gamut of theological perspective. The models are scalable for your context and can be put into motion by the folks you have in your churches. The models featured are (1) intergenerational exploratory spaces, sometimes known as "pray-grounds," (2) sensory sensitive worship practices, (3) outreach-oriented experiences, (4) church and school partnerships, and (5) contemporary worship leadership in band-led church settings. Following these models, chapter 7 offers some theological takeaways backed by research in the social sciences. The book concludes with some words of grace, a commission to do this work, and some practical steps to get you there.

I write as an ordained pastor in The United Methodist Church, a professor and theologian of worship, a parent of a young child, a musician, a qualitative researcher, and as a director of a center for worship and the arts whose purpose is to equip young disciples for faithful and artistic worship. I am not a children's ministry professional, though I am married to one.

This book emerges from countless professional conversations in which I have participated or witnessed where the engagement of children was so often framed as a mechanism to help the church's survival or growth. These conversations have not been exclusive to Mainline Protestantism. They have taken place in urban, suburban, and rural churches. They have happened in churches of all sizes and across racial demographics.

For decades, Christian education programs have been *the* solution for engaging children, especially on the Protestant side of the Christian family tree. The good news is that there is a treasure trove of literature on models of Christian education. There is such wisdom in the expertise of Christian educators, and I am grateful for the call these folks have on their lives—maybe you're one of them!

This book charts a differing path, focusing on empowering children to learn and grow as disciples in the context of corporate worship. As we will see in the various models and case studies, some of these contexts are Sunday morning, others midweek, and yet others during other established

Introduction

rhythms. Some models are "multigenerational," where all generations are present in corporate worship. Others are "intergenerational," where generations are interacting with one another with intentionality in the worship setting. And others are somewhere between.

While "age segregated" approaches to Sunday morning worship have attracted attention over the last few decades (i.e., children having their own worshiping community with dedicated content), this book will not be considering those models for two simple reasons. The first is that these models are often not scalable for the small church (under 100 people in attendance), which is nearly 70% of churches in the United States. Second, research from the Fuller Youth Institute demonstrates that young people are more likely to carry their faith into adulthood when they are nurtured in worship services with multiple generations present. None of this is to say that age-segregated models are bad, but if we are interested in forming young disciples of Jesus for lifelong faith, then let's focus our efforts on models we can sustain.

Let the Children Lead puts forth models for worship that create space for children to worship, to grow in their sense of agency, and to be nourished as lifelong disciples of Jesus Christ. Children are not numbers that ensure the survival of church institutions. That transactional model for growth has long transpired. The landscape of the Christian Church in the United States has fundamentally changed and continues to evolve.

Dear pastor or church leader, let me say this in no uncertain terms: you do not bear the sole responsibility of your church's future trajectory. I understand that numerical anxiety is real. I understand that denominational reporting metrics make us write down numbers. I understand that all too often your sense of worth as a pastor, staff member, or church ministry leader is tied to the number of butts in seats and the number of participants on paper. I lament that our denominations and bodies of accountability have not had the pastoral imagination to see vitality beyond these reporting metrics. And I know you are trying. Your labor is not in vain.

If you have been blessed with children in your congregation—whether one or one hundred—then this book is for you. These children are young worshipers whose faith lives are impacted by the witness of your churches and ministries. Regardless of the numbers of children in our programs or in the programs we desire to create, we are called to serve them with faithfulness and authenticity. I look forward to journeying with you as we explore models and takeaways that can help us do this.

Oh, and you know that church I referenced at the beginning? Well, in 2014, I got married in that church. It had a beautiful campus, was in a convenient part of town, and still felt like home. It might not have been *the* formative faith community of my childhood, but that church meant something to me. It introduced me to Jesus, and what could be more important than that?

Chapter 1
Unlearning and Reframing

In leadership and coaching books, there is a common characterization of good leaders: they are always learning. Good leaders take in new information regularly. They are naturally curious. These leaders seek the counsel and advice of others. Because of this connection between leadership and learning, a lot of ink has been spilled on the value and importance of continuing education for leaders. And let's be real, if you are reading this book, chances are that you are a person who values learning and growth in your areas of expertise and calling. I'm right there with you.

What we often fail to do in our process of learning is the intentional work of unlearning. Unlearning is a partner in the process of learning, but it requires a departure from information previously acquired.

In a book about photography, French philosopher Roland Barthes argued that every photograph signifies a type of death—the capturing of a time that will never again exist.

Though morbid sounding, this may be a helpful way to think about what to do with older models of ministry with children. These past models have been captured in time, like a photograph. They served their purpose in that moment, and it's important that we remember them. But the time in which these models worked no longer exists. We must unlearn for the sake of learning anew.

As we unlearn together, I want to help you make an argument. Well, a series of arguments. Not for the sake of being argumentative, but for

Chapter 1

the sake of the children in your context. Not just for those children, but for the caregivers and church members who love them deeply. And not just those children, caregivers, and church members, but for anyone with strong opinions about the trajectory of your church's ministry with children.

In this chapter, we will do our best to unlearn the transactional thinking that often underlies our approaches to ministry with children. We will root our unlearning in the wisdom of the Bible. Importantly, the Bible is not a photograph. While it was written in a particular time by particular people, the Holy Spirit breathes new life into the text. The scriptures are filled with insights for engaging children, helping us to both learn and unlearn.

In what follows, I offer four scripturally rooted "reframing" statements for us to consider. Maybe these phrases and redirections are for you, to aid your own process of learning and unlearning. Or perhaps you have been championing these thoughts for years but needed some concise ways to articulate them. Or maybe these are for someone in your congregation who longs to get back to the "good ol' days" when children lined the pews. Let's learn and unlearn together, looking to Jesus, the author and perfector of our faith.

From preserving the institution to advancing the Kingdom

In the minds of many, our jobs as pastors, staff members, and lay leaders is to ensure the vitality and future sustainability of our churches and ministries. These words, "vitality" and "sustainability," are often understood by our local church, denominations, and other bodies of accountability as numerically based. When numbers go up for program participation, attendance, or programming, that means we are moving toward vitality. When these numbers stagnate or falter, we are moving away from it. This can lend to a feeling of pressure that our jobs and roles depend on the numerical success and the ultimate preservation of the institution. Some of this pressure is healthy. We *should* be concerned with the health of our institutions, especially if God has called us in a time such as this to lead them.

The problem is that in the last thirty to forty years, the average churchgoer has come to believe that church vitality and programmatic success is the job of the clergy, the staff member, and the "super volunteer." In our effort to be a pragmatic people in combatting decline, the priorities of leaders have shifted, particularly of clergy. The church has adopted corporate language for the role of the pastor, that of pastor as "Chief Executive Officer." And if the pastor is like a CEO, that means the C-Suite (COO, CFO, CIO, etc.) is the church staff team and those faithfully dedicated volunteers. And if we have a CEO and a C-Suite, that means your average congregant fits the role of consumer.

I am not saying that we have actively disempowered the laity and made them consumers. There was not a secret town hall meeting that insidiously revoked their leadership privileges. However, I am saying that the increased professionalization of ministry has created the necessary conditions for your average churchgoer to feel like the stakes are lower for them. The resulting mentality often sounds something like, "Why do I need to give up my time to volunteer in the children's ministry if we have dedicated professionals for this? This is why I give some of my money, right?"

If we are not careful, this professionalization of ministry can lead us to an implicit goal: preserving the institution rather than nurturing the life of the Kingdom.

Jesus has opinions about this.

In Mark 10, after teaching on divorce and offering a subversive strengthening of Mosaic law, Jesus models another act of intrigue: welcoming the children in his midst. Women and children did not hold much power in the first century, which is evident by how poorly they were treated by Jesus's disciples (Mark 10:13). Jesus admonished these disciples and instead invited the children to come to him. People on society's margins of power were centered. In fact, Jesus declared that the Kingdom of God belonged especially to people who were like children.

This passage says many things about the nature of God. In addition to the hospitality Jesus models, and in addition to his challenging teaching that we must "receive the kingdom of God as a little child," we learn that Jesus was not a big fan of preserving institutions and institutional ideas for the sake of the institution. His most steadfast antagonists were institutionalists who were upset and threatened by his reinterpretation of the law. Those looking to Jesus for validation of institutional preservation may find less support than expected.

In reframing our theological approach to ministry with children, we would do well to remember that Jesus told the children to "come to me," not "come to the Church." Although our local churches are beautiful sites of God's activity, institutions come and go. The Church is not the Kingdom of God, but it is invited to be a vehicle through which God's Kingdom is ushered in.

In our ministry with children, how can we cast a vision of Kingdom flourishing?

What if we prioritized introducing children to Jesus rather than to our local church?

What if we cared more about the vitality of the Kingdom instead of the vitality of our local church programs?

This does not mean that the local church is unimportant—far from it! However, Jesus knows how susceptible we are of making an idol out of institutions and metrics. When we make the subtle, but critical shift of orienting our ministries toward Kingdom flourishing, the children in our care will be better served. And at the end of the day, isn't that the point? Our goal isn't just to nurture children who know how to participate in church programs—it's to form disciples who know and follow Jesus, whether or not they stay in our particular pews.

From numerical economics to numerical blessing

How many children does it take before we decide to invest in their spiritual formation? At what point do we deem a ministry "worth it"?

The first church I served had an average worship attendance of 30. We had two children in our care—siblings. On Sunday mornings, we offered a Sunday school class for those two children, led by two faithful Christian educators. During the worship service, we also hired nursery workers who, more often than not, spent the next hour chatting amongst themselves with no babies in their care.

Coming from a large church background, I remember thinking how inefficient this sounded. The Sunday School teachers always had a hard time recruiting their replacements when they were away. I was skeptical of us buying new curriculum when we had a treasure trove of curriculum from the "glory days" of the church's children's ministry. On top of this, we were spending money each week to pay nursery workers to tend to an empty room. I was unable to see clearly the value of investing all this time and resources for two children. Thankfully, I heeded the common advice given to first time pastors: try not to change anything too drastically your first year.

I was guilty of something many of us are: the temptation to be guided by rational economic thinking when it comes to our ministries with children. Some of us flock to strategies of scarcity, while others think solely of future abundance. In a scarcity approach, we may not see the value in recruiting more volunteers. We may not think critically about the curriculum we're using in Christian education or the ways that we empower children in corporate worship. We are always wondering if we have a "critical mass" of children for it to be worth the investment.

On the other end of the spectrum, some of us believe that we must build children's ministries that anticipate future growth. If we make that early investment in a volunteer base, in curriculum, in staffing, in space and materials, then all that momentum will generate numerical abundance. This strategy of future abundance is a repackaged version of "if we build it, they will come," a mentality conditioned by the church growth movement of the latter half of the twentieth century. That is no longer a viable model for most of our churches.

The scarcity approach and the abundance approach both have their rational economic advantages, but they are in tension with what Jesus calls us to do: bless the children in our midst. When people brought their children to Jesus in Mark 10, he did not question the number of children, nor the motives of the caregivers who accompanied them. Jesus celebrated their presence, laid his hands on them, and blessed them.

If we are interested in ministry with children *for the sake* of the Kingdom of God (and not the institutional church), then perhaps we can take comfort in another metaphor Jesus offers. In describing this Kingdom, he often uses agricultural images, and most often, seeds. Seeds take time. They require tending and care. But when the time comes for seeds to germinate and grow, the end result puts God's beauty and faithfulness on full display. Similarly, we are called to care for the children in our midst, recognizing that we may not get to witness for ourselves the ways God works in their lives nor in the life of the church in the long term.

The rational economics of scarcity and future abundance are just that, rational. For instance, it's not a bad thing to be concerned about the appropriate use of time and resources. Moreover, it's not bad to be optimistic about the future growth of your ministry with children. However, when we spend too much time focusing on this scarcity or this future abundance, we can forget what Jesus has modeled for us: we have been richly blessed with the children in front of us. It may be one or two children or it may be forty or fifty. If we are faithful with the numerical blessing of children we already have, then perhaps we might be fit for even greater responsibility in the future.

From spoon-feeding their faith to respecting their agency

My call to pastoral ministry became clear at a Starbucks on my university's campus. As a student leader of a United Methodist campus ministry in the U.S. South, I often met with students who had big questions about Christianity. Having gone through my own experience of theological unlearning and relearning as a high schooler, I was drawn to these students. Many of them had strong biblical literacy but were never given space to ask questions in their churches of origin. Many attended worship services but were never invited into any form of leadership. These students came from diverse denominations and church sizes—there was no single "type" of church or leader among them. They had, however, been spoon-fed their faith.

Spoon-feeding is not inherently bad, of course. I have fond memories of spoon-feeding real food to my daughter when she was a baby, and even today, she still demands that I feed her—especially when it's a food she does not prefer (I do not often oblige—cultivating agency and grit, right?).

There are seasons to spoon-feeding faith. In James Fowler's groundbreaking book *Stages of Faith*, he describes stage one of faith as "Intuitive-Projective Faith," where children—roughly of preschool age—make sense of their faith from parents, guardians, or other significant adults in their lives. In stage two, "Mythic-Literal Faith," children ages 6 to 12 are able to think more for themselves in concrete ways, so their faith centers stories and embodied experiences. The end of stage two is usually when the spoon-feeding subsides. Faith typically becomes "one's own" between the ages of 13 and 18, which is stage three in Fowler's schema. However, even in this stage, faith remains closely tied to one's family.

Fowler's stages can be helpful tools for designing curriculum and programming. However, sometimes when we focus too much on helping young people move from one stage to the next, we forget to pause and recognize the gift of each stage. Every child is an expert in their own experiences, including *their* faith. If the Bible says that the Kingdom belongs to those who are "like" children, then why do we often treat children as non-experts in matters of faith?

One of my favorite passages of the Bible is a nightmare for parents, but a fantastic story about agency and curiosity. It's about young Jesus in the Gospel of Luke, chapter 2. When he was twelve years old, Jesus and his family went to Jerusalem for the Festival of the Passover. When the festival was over and they were making their way back home, Jesus somehow slipped away from his parents. Then, verse 46 says, "After three days they found him in the temple, sitting among the teachers, listening to them and asking them questions." Can you imagine your child being lost for three days?!

The striking feature of this story is that Jesus feels comfortable enough in the temple to sit down and ask questions of the religious leaders. While Jesus's communications skills with his parents leave something to be desired, he models agency and curiosity. The passage continues by reporting that everyone was amazed at the level of understanding in his questions and answers.

We likely won't have any repeat instances of young Jesus in our congregations, but we are serving those who are made in his image. Are we creating space for their curiosity? Are we allowing the youngest disciples to be experts in their own experiences, while also pointing them to the richness of the gospel?

If the Kingdom belongs to those who are like children, then let's honor their agency and foster their curiosity—spoon-feeding when appropriate, but ultimately shaping a faith that is truly their own.

From Sunday instruction to Monday faith

Is Sunday the encapsulation of the week behind us? Or is Sunday the beginning of a new week? How do you view this day in your life rhythm?

Traditionally, we have been taught that Sunday is the first day of the week, highlighting its intended importance in the broader society. We can see this in the physical layout of our calendars, which are commonly structured Sunday to Saturday. In practice, though, Sunday can often feel like a final day of freedom before the beginning of a work week.

The theological tradition of the Church teaches us that Sunday is both the first day and the "eighth day." It is the first day insofar as it mirrors God's work in the creation of the world, where God created light and separated it from darkness. Additionally, this first day marks both the resurrection of Jesus and the giving of the Holy Spirit at Pentecost. What better time to celebrate God's goodness than the first day of the week?

At the same time, Sunday is also regarded as the "eighth day," which is rooted in the Jewish apocalyptic tradition. Over the centuries, Christians have come to understand the eighth day as a sign of the new creation, the time when God sets the world right in Jesus Christ—where the Kingdom he so frequently proclaimed comes in its fullness. The importance of the eighth day is why many baptismal fonts are eight-sided and why folks like John Wesley—the co-founder of Methodism—designed chapels to be eight-sided. This bears witness to the fact that in Christ, we are already a new creation, even as we await the fullness of God's renewal.

The reality of Sunday as both the first day and the eighth day teaches us that in between those days, we have a lot of work to do. So why do we often treat Sundays as the "be-all and end-all" of the formation of children?

For many families, Sunday is no longer a sacred day set apart for worship—it competes with sports, errands, and other obligations. This shift is reflected in recent Gallup polling (2021–2023), which shows that while 44% of Protestant churchgoers attend worship almost every week, another 40% attend just once per month or less, and 16% never attend at all. If nearly half of Protestant churchgoers attend sporadically or never, then our ministries cannot depend on Sunday worship alone to form young disciples. How closely are we paying attention to these rhythms in the planning of our ministries with children?

In the sixth chapter of Deuteronomy, Moses impresses upon the people of Israel the importance of internalizing the commandments of the Lord. After sharing the Ten Commandments, Moses implores them:

> Keep these words that I am commanding you today in your heart. Recite them to your children and *talk about them when you are at home* and when you are away, *when you lie down and when you rise*. Bind them *as a sign on your hand*, fix them *as an emblem on your forehead*, and *write them on the doorposts of your house* and on your gates.

This is not Moses saying, "sit and listen," now "go and do." What we have is a multisensory approach that reinforces learning and identity throughout the week. There are conversations in the family being held,

Chapter 1

there are recitations at fixed times, there are reminders on our bodies, and there are physical signs in our homes. There is deep wisdom here.

In our own contexts, perhaps we have given too much emphasis on Sunday when it comes to discipling our youngest worshipers. If families are attending worship once or twice per month, there is no way a one-hour service and maybe a Sunday school lesson can "do the work" of formation. Like Moses and the children of Israel, we need a multi-pronged strategy.

We have precedent in richness in our own history, though. Something the Protestant Reformation did well was to reinforce the rhythms of Sunday worship in the family unit throughout the week. Formation was not solely the church's job—it was a shared practice, woven into the fabric of home life. Usually offered twice per day—morning and evening—families practiced their faith through prayer, scripture readings, and the singing of psalms and hymns.

Sunday as a set-apart day is less and less the reality in our society. Rather than fighting culture wars to reclaim its importance, how are we equipping our children and families for this reality? If Sunday is both "first day" and the "eighth day," then what we do—and what we offer—on Monday through Saturday matters. How much does our programming and curriculum revolve around Sunday? What might we need to adjust? How might we supplement this with other on-ramps for children and families?

If our ministries are truly oriented toward the flourishing of God's Kingdom, then our discipleship must extend beyond Sunday—shaping faith not just in the church, but in the rhythms of daily life.

Shifting Our Focus

The way we shape our ministries reflects what we truly value. As a reminder, the "transactional" model of ministry is when churches or ministries make intentional programmatic changes with the hoped-for outcome of increased attendance, participation, or commitment to the organization. This chapter has shown how the transactional model prioritizes institutional survival over Kingdom flourishing. It wants us to obsess over numbers, allowing us to forget the blessing of the children already in our midst. For ease of programming, this model prioritizes the transmission of content in neat and tidy ways rather than creating space for children to exhibit agency and lean into curiosity. And it focuses so much on Sunday morning as the principal time of formation that it neglects the other days of the week.

In unlearning this transactional model that's been pervasive over the last 75 years or more, nuance is important. We can and should love our local churches. We can and should want to see programming be the best that it can. We can and should want our churches to survive for decades and centuries to come. But when it comes to the formation of children, the health of the local church cannot be what we value the most. The transactional model excelled when the church was at the center of society. That time has come and gone.

We are instead invited to shift our focus to models that center children and families, investing in their faith formation that is oriented toward the flourishing of the Kingdom. Sometimes implementing this shift can be disruptive and even countercultural to the local church. It challenges deeply ingrained assumptions about success and sustainability. Starting or refining ministries that are not squarely interested in adding butts to seats and numbers to rolls can be a steep uphill race. It is a risk worth taking.

As we continue to learn and unlearn, the following chapters will highlight models of worship-based ministry with children from churches that have taken Kingdom-minded risks. These models and case studies are intended to inspire creativity in your local context. They are not quick fixes. In fact, most of them take significant time to develop and all of them require a level of investment that prioritizes faithfulness over efficiency—at least by the standards of our denominations, networks, and accountability structures.

What they *will* do is center children and families, welcoming them, nurturing their gifts, and equipping them for a life of discipleship—just like Jesus modeled for us.

Chapter 2
Pray-Grounds

> "All are welcome."
> *Moments later...*
> "Children, you are dismissed."

For the last few decades, churches across the United States have made decisions about children in worship based on what seems most *manageable* rather than what is most *faithful*. This often reflects generational assumptions. We make decisions that center adults and their preferences for an enjoyable worship experience. Sometimes this results in the separation of age groups where, as indicated in the quotation above, children are separated from the adult worshiping community and segmented into their own. In other congregations, this pragmatism can show up as a "children's moment," where children are invited forward for a brief lesson in front of the congregation, then return to their seats.

Neither approach is inherently wrong—we want children to be engaged. However, both scenarios communicate that there is a *specific time and place* for children to be engaged in worship. Instead of seeing children as full participants, we risk treating them as visitors to a space that ultimately belongs to adults.

Worship is the work of all God's people. It should be our goal to make every component of the worship service accessible to all generations. As a pastor, I often hear from adults how meaningful a "children's moment"

Chapter 2

can be, even though they are not the intended audience—and I believe them! Children's moments often make difficult concepts quite accessible. So, why do we think the reverse would not be true? Children can and do find meaning in the "adult" parts of the worship service. They sing, they pray, they move their bodies, they interact with other people. And even in the most "adult" component of worship—the sermon—they are listening even when we think they are not. The whole service is for them.

What if, instead, we were called to center our youngest disciples boldly? If children are worshipers alongside every generation, then our focus should not be on carving out a moment that appeals to them or sending them elsewhere for a more "age-appropriate" experience. Instead, what if we removed the barriers that keep them on the margins and reimagined worship as a space where their agency is fully assumed? How do we cultivate an environment throughout the entire worship service in which children and their families feel empowered to sing, to dance, to pray, to create, to play? This is not a minor programming adjustment; it is a cultural shift—one that calls upon the whole congregation to foreground children, to embrace their wisdom and their messiness, and to join together in the work of all God's people.

Many churches seeking to embody this shift have found the journey to be uphill, but one approach that has gained traction is the creation of a pray-ground in the sanctuary.

Pray-Grounds

While set-apart spaces for children have existed for a long time, the concept of a pray-ground went social media "viral" among many pastors and leaders in 2016. A pray-ground is often described as an intentional space, typically in the front of the sanctuary, set apart for children and their families to worship in age-appropriate ways alongside the rest of the community. By creating an environment that feels familiar to children—with furnishings that meet their stature and materials that signify creativity, playfulness, and reverence—pray-grounds lower the barrier of participation for children. This allows them to worship alongside the rest of the congregation in ways that are sensitive to their developmental needs.

Our physical worship spaces are not obviously hospitable to children. There are pews or chairs tailored to adult bodies; there are sometimes restrictions about food and drink; there are many objects in our sanctuaries that look fascinating but should not be touched. Imagine being a child walking into this a space vastly different from those they navigate throughout the week.

For perspective, I like to think of this in the inverse. When I visit a preschool classroom or any classroom that is for elementary-aged children or younger, my body immediately knows that this space is *not for me*. It's almost visceral. The tables and chairs are too small and will not support my weight. There are books not commensurate with my reading level. The décor does not match my vibe. When I walk into a space like this, I do not imagine it as a place where I can spend time and comfortably engage in age-appropriate activities. The same is often true for children in our spaces.

Pray-grounds commonly feature a rug or series of rugs that set the space apart, child-friendly seating, a table (or multiple), and quiet books, toys, and other creative materials for them to use in worship. They can be as simple or as elaborate as your church's liturgical space allows.

Pray-grounds are opportunities for leaders to be intentional about how the space should be outfitted. For example, there could be specific toys and activities that are appropriate for a particular liturgical season or civic observance. It could also be used to reinforce or supplement curriculum that takes place in the context of Sunday School or other intentional children's programming. Or if you have a particularly musical congregation that doesn't mind a little bit of joyously discordant sound or rhythm—consider musical instruments!

Ultimately, the pray-ground is what you make of it. Let's now turn to two congregations to see how they have implemented pray-grounds in their contexts over the years.

Chapter 2

Case Study #1 – Pray-Grounds and a Church Merger
Radiance Community Church (Roanoke, VA)

On the outskirts of Roanoke, Virginia, two churches recently came together to launch a new congregation as a part of the Cooperative Baptist Fellowship denomination. The average worship attendance at Radiance Community Church is approximately 70 people on Sunday mornings, with anywhere between three and ten children attending each week. I had the opportunity to speak with Rev. Melissa Scott, one of the current co-pastors. Prior to this merger, she served as Associate Pastor for Families and later became Senior Pastor of one of the predecessor churches, Colonial Avenue Baptist Church.

In 2017, as Associate Pastor for Families at Colonial Avenue Baptist Church, Melissa had the idea of implementing a pray-ground, which emerged from both practical and theological considerations. Melissa explains, "Part of it was a practical matter—I didn't know if I had enough volunteers. The bigger piece for me was theological, because I believe that we need each other generationally."

With decades of Christian education experience under her belt, she felt strongly that children should be active participants in the worship service. "I think children learn to worship by *being* in worship, and I think that children teach *us adults* about worship by being in worship," she states. When pray-grounds started making the headlines in 2016 and 2017, Melissa recalls reaching out to other clergy who had implemented them in their contexts. With some intentional teaching to the congregation and the public buy-in from her senior pastor, Melissa was able to both show and tell how the pray-ground would be a faithful witness to intergenerational worship.

Melissa's approach to pray-grounds is hands-on and interactive. She often functioned as a "worship host," sitting with the children and guiding them through various worship activities. "When we're singing, I would have ribbons for worship movements so that they were moving their bodies. The same with prayers of the people: we were always doing something hands-on to pray," she explains. The role of worship host keeps the children active, helps them learn the rhythms and practices of worship, and frees up the direct caregivers to worship in their own way.

The implementation of pray-grounds has not been without challenges. Melissa shared that the COVID-19 pandemic led to a re-launch of the pray-ground, with many children having to adjust behaviorally to being in community once again. Additionally, the merger of the two churches brought new dynamics, as the other predecessor church had not had children in its congregation for a long time. Despite these hurdles, Melissa remained committed to her intergenerational vision of worship, adapting and evolving the pray-ground to meet the needs of the congregation.

One of the most profound impacts of the pray-ground has been the way it fosters relationships within the church. Melissa shares, "Because the children are there, that means that they're right there after worship as well, and so folks get to know them and they get to know the adults in the church who care for them, and they learn each other's names in a way that they wouldn't necessarily do if they were not right there."

The pray-ground has also provided opportunities for children to express their faith and emotions. Melissa recounts a touching moment when a young girl responded to the music during Lent, saying, "I don't like this music. It makes me sad." This interaction led to a beautiful conversation about the season of Lent and the significance of how this sadness resolves in the victory of Jesus Christ over sin and death.

For Rev. Melissa Scott and her church, the pray-ground has shown her just how much kids are listening to the worship service and how the words of scripture and the words of the church's liturgy are getting into the bones of these youngest disciples. "When I hear the children begin to be able to speak the words of the liturgy for the first time, it's a beautiful thing, knowing that they're picking up those pieces," she explains.

Colonial Avenue Baptist Church, and later, Radiance Community Church, have been firsthand witnesses of God's faithfulness in the lives of the children and families. Melissa summarily reflects, "The pray-ground has allowed us to see the beauty of worship through the eyes of our children, enriching our entire congregation."

Chapter 2

Case Study #2 – Pray-grounds in a Multicultural Context
South Church (New Britain, CT)

South Church is a congregation of the United Church of Christ and the American Baptist Churches nestled in the heart of New Britain, Connecticut. The pastor, Rev. Jane Rowe, describes the area as an urban environment with a rich cultural, racial, and economic tapestry. Despite its grandiose Early English Gothic architecture and the church's historical ties to white and affluent community members, South Church has evolved to include a wide range of backgrounds and experiences, reflecting the broader community of New Britain. On a typical Sunday, South Church has 60 to 80 people in worship, including 1 to 6 children.

The idea for the pray-ground emerged as a practical solution when the church struggled to sustain its age-segmented model during worship. Now that children were back in the sanctuary for the full service, many families felt like their young children were not engaged during worship. With a background in intergenerational children's ministry, Jane led a quick discernment process, supported by a webinar training from Practical Resources for Churches (PRC), then launched its pray-ground as an experiment in the summer of 2023.

Choosing the location for the pray-ground within the sanctuary was a process of trial and error. Initially, the church tried placing it up front in the middle section of the sanctuary but quickly realized that it wasn't the best spot. "Parents felt way too exposed, and other congregation members felt like it posed too much of a distraction," Jane explains. The pray-ground was then moved to the right side of the sanctuary—still up front—which provided a more comfortable and practical space for both children and parents. "It's a better spot all around," Jane notes, adding that the new location allowed for bookcases, a quieter environment, and a nearby door for an easy exit.

South Church's pray-ground is mostly self-directed. Each week, a key children's ministry volunteer curates a creative activity for the pray-ground that ties in with the central scripture passage, setting up materials, instructions, and.even a completed model in advance. Parents and caregivers then guide their children through these activities. In addition to the guided activities, there are three small tables, about eight chairs, a few rugs to contain the space and dampen sound, books, and other activity sheets with crayons and writing utensils.

The initial experiment of the pray-ground worked. One of the key successes has been its ability to make families feel more comfortable and welcome in the church. Jane shares a touching story about a young boy who grew to love the pray-ground so much that he replicated it for online worship. When he watches the service from home, he turns on a battery-operated candle, mimicking the lighting of the Christ candle in the sanctuary. "It moves me every time I see it. He totally gets it. He can do this from home as well as when he's with us in worship," she says.

However, the implementation of pray-grounds has not been without its challenges. Even with the location change, noise levels have regularly been a concern. The church has worked to balance the needs of the congregation with the presence of children, encouraging both parents and other worshipers to adapt. "The congregation also needs to learn that it's up to them to not be distracted," Jane advises.

The pray-ground has become a beloved feature of the church, providing a space where children can feel involved and valued. While not without challenges, it has created a more inclusive and engaging worship experience for families.

Benefits and Challenges

As you discern whether a pray-ground may be a good model for your programming with children in worship, consider the following benefits and challenges.

Benefits

- **Children up Front |** The physical space of the church can reveal a lot about the priorities of a congregation. One of the greatest benefits of a pray-ground is the theological symbolism of children up front, participating in worship. This signifies that children are viewed as important co-worshipers with all other ages in the congregation—not an afterthought or a problem to be remedied. There is a set-apart space for them so that they can learn how to be worshipers alongside the other generations present.

- **Enhancing a Children's Moment** | For congregations that use a "children's moment" in the order of service, the pray-ground can be an excellent location for that. Pastors and leaders can be intentional about tailoring that moment with appropriate materials.

- **Opportunities for Intergenerational Preaching** | The location of the pray-ground makes it easier for the preacher to speak directly to children during the sermon. Although this style of preaching may not be for everyone, it is an easy way to speak directly to these youngest disciples in the context of intergenerational worship. In addition to incorporating relevant examples to the lives of children during the sermon, the preacher could also include creative prompts, such as "draw a picture of __," or "build a __ using the foam blocks."

- **Balancing Worship and Play** | Children get to practice and learn the ins and outs of the worship service while also having the option to "check out" and play. By having a space dedicated to worshipping as a child, this can make worship as a weekly event feel like less pressure.

- **Church Member Involvement** | There are ample opportunities for church members to furnish the pray-ground and steward its care. They could supply or create toys, donate books and oversee their rotation, clean and sanitize the space, and even take turns "hosting" the pray-ground each week. When church members feel a sense of responsibility, they're more likely to invest in its success.

Challenges

- **Noisy and Distracting** | One of the most obvious challenges is noise and distracting behaviors. When two or more children gather, there will be noise. This can be minimized through the selection of proper materials, limiting seats, and providing clear guidelines for parents and guardians. However, some will still view their mere presence up front as a distraction. This critique offers an opportunity for intentional teaching—expanding people's understandings of reverence. Alternatively, you can gently encourage people to sit in a different area of the worship space that is not in direct sightlines of the pray-ground.

- **Timeliness Challenges for Families** | The location up front is a great physical example of our theological commitment to children, but it may not always be practical for families who are juggling many priorities that have them arriving late to the service. When the space is in front of the congregation, latecomers with children may be hesitant to walk all the way to the front.

- **Supervision Required** | Pray-grounds are not a "set it and forget it" activity. In fact, they often require *more* supervision from parents than if children were sitting with their families in chairs. This is where a pray-ground "host" can be beneficial, so that a lay leader can guide children through the service.

- **Real Estate is Precious** | It's great that church members feel ownership over the church's physical space, but sometimes this may devolve into territorialism. Carving out liturgical real estate involves multiple stakeholders, including intentional teaching with strong biblical and theological support.

- **Aesthetics** | Unsurprisingly, people have opinions about furnishings and the tidiness of the space. Some may suggest that the "kidlike" nature of the pray-ground is an eyesore to

Chapter 2

an otherwise beautiful space. You'll need to have conversations and policies about what to do with the pray-ground for events like weddings and funerals.

Next Steps

Implementing a pray-ground can transform your church's approach to intergenerational worship. Here's how to do it well.

As with implementing any kind of new program, you will first want to solicit buy-in from families and church leadership teams. Cast the vision to them and the entire congregation: all generations need one another in worship, and children's faith is as much caught as it is taught. Highlight the practical benefits, such as opportunities for volunteering, the greater visibility of children, and hospitality to guests who may be nervous to bring children to church. For families who opt out of a Sunday School option, the pray-ground might be one of their few opportunities to worship and meet other families with children.

On the church finance side, this is a great way to encourage a donor who is passionate about the formation of children. Depending on your liturgical space and the materials selected for the pray-ground, this can be a very low-cost endeavor.

Think strategically about materials. One go-to feature that is widely reported among churches with pray-grounds is a set of foam blocks. They encourage creativity, are low on the noise level, can be shared for cooperative play, and are easily sanitized. Coloring sheets or blank pages of paper are another staple, along with crayons or washable markers stored in a cloth basket. Bibles and books are a must, but consider offering just a few options each week, and regularly rotate them. Any materials that can be used with minimal adult intervention and minimal noise are excellent choices for the pray-ground.

Consider implementing a trial period. Sometimes "new" is not so scary if it's framed as a fixed amount of time or an experiment. I recommend a period of three to six months. This should be preceded by intentional teaching from the pulpit, whether as part of a sermon series, the children's time, or with some strategic announcements. When you have designed and built out your pray-ground, pre-select some families to commit to using it each week. It will not be compelling visual imagery if no one is using the space.

Your church will need to establish clear guidelines about the pray-ground. For example, parents or caregivers should stay nearby to help redirect when needed. While full participation in worship is encouraged, expectations for noise levels should be communicated. Provide clear instructions on materials—what's available, how to use them, and cleanup expectations. You can have these guidelines printed and clearly available for families. Alternatively, a volunteer "worship host" can share the guidelines verbally just before the service.

Finally, criticism is to be expected. Equip leaders with simple, pastoral responses. If someone says, "It's too distracting," remind them that children are part of the body of Christ or invite them to sit in an area of the church that's not in direct sightlines. If there are noise complaints (there will be), acknowledge the challenge but affirm that joyful noise belongs in worship and how blessed we are to have multiple generations present. Overall, emphasize the church's commitment to intergenerational worship. Thoughtful responses can help shift the conversation from complaint to shared vision.

One Tool in a Larger Toolbox

In writing this book, I also had the opportunity to speak with Evangelical Lutheran Church in America (ELCA) pastor, Rev. Andrea Roske-Metcalfe, who is often credited with being the founder of the pray-grounds movement. She still writes, teaches, and consults on pray-grounds. In my conversation with her, she offered a piece of wisdom that is an excellent concluding word. Rev. Roske-Metcalfe shared that pray-grounds are not the consummate solution to engaging children in worship. They should be one piece in a "constellation of options" to better incorporate children into the worshiping life of the community.

Pray-grounds are not a silver bullet to the full inclusion of children's participation in worship, nor can one program check all the boxes for liturgical formation. But they are a tangible, visible commitment to the theological truth that children *belong*—not on the margins, not completely siloed into their own space, but at the heart of the worshiping community. Pray-grounds teach us that faith is both taught and caught, that children can worship in age-appropriate ways alongside adults, and that congregations can recognize the gift of intergenerational worship if they open themselves up to the Spirit's leading.

Worship is the work of all God's people. Implementing a pray-ground is one way your church could live that out.

Resources to Engage

Visit abingdonpress.com/children-lead-extras for additional information and links to the following resources.

Worship Woodworks
Wooden products depicting Bible stories.

Godly Play Store
Resources related to the Godly Play program (often in Episcopal Churches), featuring tactile objects and devotional resources for children.

Webinar: Praygrounds and Worship Activities for Children
Produced by Practical Resources for Churches (PRC) and led by Christine V. Hides, an expert in Christian education and a deacon in The United Methodist Church.

Chapter 3
Sensory Sensitive Worship

Over the centuries, the Church's worship has been marked by the embrace of technology. From building towering sanctuaries for reverberant sound, to the construction of pews for orderly seating, to the use of wireless microphones and LED walls, our worship has changed as technology has advanced. In my pastoral experience, changes in worship technology are often met with skepticism until the benefits become clear. For example, adding a projector screen to the sanctuary may seem like an eyesore to some, but it may also lead to increased visibility, new ways of incorporating visual dimensions of worship, or the sustainability benefit of having a paper-free worship service.

Over these same centuries, technological and scientific advancements have allowed us to learn more about the human body—be it basic anatomy and physiology, how illness and diseases spread, what makes us tick on a cellular level, to the intricacies of our brains and emotions. In worship, for example, the discovery of germs and the knowledge of how disease spreads have taught us to be mindful of hand hygiene, as well as the importance of staying home when sick. Our evolving understanding of physical disabilities has taught us to be intentional with architectural designs and church renovations to ensure accessibility. It's also very likely our preaching and approaches to pastoral care have changed now that we understand the magnitude of the mental health crisis.

Chapter 3

Worship is embodied. But sometimes, when it's not *our* bodies that are negatively affected by the Church's worship, then we do not pay as much attention to those whose are. Making changes to accommodate "the few" can feel unjustified or even unfair to "the many." And yet, we follow a savior whose heart is to leave the ninety-nine when seeking out the one.

Over the last several years, there has been increased attention to "sensory sensitive" approaches in worship. The Church's worship on Sunday morning is a sensory rich environment—lights, sounds, tastes, smells, all combined with physical interactions with other people. Worship can feel overwhelming for many and can lead to sensory overload. For those who may be neurotypical or do not experience sensory sensitivities, one can easily be dismissive of this or believe it may affect a small minority of people. However, those with sensory sensitivities in worship make up a much larger swath of our church population than we might assume.

Coined in the mid-1990s by psychologists Elaine and Arthur Aron, *Sensory Processing Sensitivity* (SPS) is a biologically based trait characterized by heightened responsiveness to physical, emotional, social, or environmental stimuli—often paired with an orientation to a rich inner life. Aron and Aron estimate that this trait appears in approximately 15 to 20% of the population. Although commonly observed in individuals with diagnoses such as ADHD, autism, anxiety, or PTSD, SPS is an independent trait that may or may not accompany such diagnoses.

In other words, people with SPS are not an obscure subgroup within our congregations—they're a significant part of our worshiping body. According to KultureCity, one of the leading non-profit organizations in sensory sensitivity, that number is closer to one in four. These are children, youth, and adults in our churches week after week. How can the church be more welcoming to nearly one quarter of its worshiping population?

A quick aside before we go any further. In writing this chapter, I feel the need to confess that I have perfectionistic tendencies. As a reader of books like these, I carry within me the temptation to digest all these helpful models and approaches to ministry and go "all in." If you resonate with this in the slightest, it's best for me to offer an important caveat for this chapter: there is no "perfect" way of being a sensory sensitive congregation. However, if you have children who attend worship with all generations present, there will be *some* clear things you can implement to serve a portion of your worshiping population.

Sensory Sensitive Worship

Sensory sensitive worship is not as much a "model" for engaging children in worship as it is an approach to worship hospitality. But before we can extend the hospitality of Christ to folks with sensory processing differences, we need to understand the unique ways God has created these beloved ones.

In her excellent guide to churches, *Worship Without Limits: Practical Guidance for Ministry Leaders Shepherding Individuals with Sensory Sensitivity,* Samford University psychology professor Dr. Amanda Howard articulates five characteristics of people with sensory sensitivity that are relevant to their participation in the church: (1) a heightened sense of empathy and compassion for the needs of others, (2) an appreciation for beauty, art, and symbolism, (3) a reflective and introspective nature, (4) a good sense of perception to notice nuances and subtleties in their surroundings, and (5) a commitment to authenticity and sincerity. By recognizing these gifts, we are not just accommodating needs but creating space for the gifts of sensory-sensitive worshipers to flourish.

Dr. Howard's resource guide is anchored in robust research. In a survey with 1,322 people (702 adults with sensory sensitivity, 514 parents of children with sensory sensitivity, and 106 ministry leaders), here are some of the top challenges reported by people with sensory sensitivity:

- Prolonged periods of sitting or standing (39.8%)
- Lengthy prayers or rituals (36.1%)
- Loud music/singing/clapping (33.8%)
- Confined or crowded spaces (32.2%)
- Large crowds (29.9%)

Chapter 3

- Too much social interaction (28.1%)

These sensory challenges resulted in feelings of:

- Overwhelm (48.6%)
- Stress (38%)
- Disconnection from the worship experience (36.1%)
- Exhaustion (32.2%)
- Perceived judgment by the congregation (22.3%)
- Isolation (18.2%).

These reported feelings led to a variety of behavioral responses, including

- Attending services less frequently (47.8%)
- Avoiding certain services (32.3%)
- Leaving early or arriving late (28.5%)
- Seeking alternative ways to engage with their faith (28.1%)
- Decreasing level of participation during services (26.9%)
- Stopping attending altogether (14.1%)

Recognizing the gifts and the challenges of sensory sensitive people should encourage churches to reassess their worship services and their overall approach to hospitality. While there are a variety of ways to welcome and affirm sensory sensitive people, the four major approaches involve (1) creating space, (2) providing comforting objects and materials, (3) raising awareness through intentional teaching, and (4) being liturgically flexible. These can all be implemented in varying degrees and stages.

The first is creating a sensory friendly space within the church. Ideally, this space is near the sanctuary for easy access during worship if anyone needs a break from the sensory stimuli in the service. The lighting is lower in these spaces, the livestream of the service is at a comfortable volume, and there are flexible seating options. It is important that this space is not shared as a "cry room" for infants, as this can defeat the purpose of having a quiet, calming space.

The second is providing sensory friendly objects and materials. The following table offers some recommendations based on the sensory processing route.

Auditory	Tactile	Visual	Olfactory
Noise-cancelling headphones	Fidget toys	Sunglasses	Scratch-and-sniff cards
Audio stories	Playdough	Calming visual aids	Scented markers
Soothing music	Squishy toys	Kaleidoscope	Balms or lotions
	Weighted stuffed animal		

You can create a sensory bag and pre-stock it with a variety of these items, or you can keep these items in clearly labeled bins and allow children and their families to select their items. If the church has a designated sensory room, many of these items should also be stocked there.

The third approach to sensory sensitive worship is cultivating empathy through intentional teaching. Sharing openly about the resources your church uses to welcome folks with sensory sensitivities helps families feel more welcome, equips neurotypical church members to have a greater understanding of their fellow worshipers, all of which contributes to reducing stigma and to the full embrace of all people in worship.

Modeling flexibility in worship services is the fourth way to welcome children with sensory sensitivity. Some churches have the capability of adding a sensory-sensitive service, while others may make congregation-wide adjustments (loudness/style of music, lighting decisions, seating arrangements) to better accommodate sensory sensitive worshipers.

Engaging sensory sensitive worshipers involves listening deeply to your context. So far, this chapter has made little mention of children, which speaks to how sensory sensitive worship is inherently intergenerational. The next case studies, however, are of churches that are offering exemplary ministries at various scales particularly with children.

Chapter 3

Case Study #1 – Sensory Friendly Intergenerational Worship

Cross of Peace Lutheran Church (Shakopee, MN)

On the outskirts of Minneapolis, Minnesota, Cross of Peace Lutheran Church welcomes about 80 worshipers each Sunday, with a congregation that skews younger. It has become a haven for young people on the autism spectrum, many of whom have sensory processing sensitivity. Their church mission statement? "Welcoming all and sharing God's love across the spectrum." However, this missional focus on serving families, especially families of young people with autism, is relatively new.

The inspiration for their sensory-friendly services has a surprising origin: a sermon series on Netflix shows. During a sermon about *Atypical*—a show following an autistic teenager's journey—Pastor Stephanie invited a speaker to discuss how churches can better welcome children on the spectrum. "It really got us thinking about how we could better serve these families," she recounts. Cross of Peace already had many young families with children, including those on the autism spectrum. With the added benefit of its modern construction without the standard "church smell," Cross of Peace was poised to serve this community in a transformative way.

Cross of Peace has thoughtfully designed its worship services to accommodate the needs of individuals with sensory sensitivities. Upon entering the church, worshipers can pick up social scripts. If you're unfamiliar with a social script, it is a pictorial guide with simple annotations of the church's worship experience. At Cross of Peace, these scripts are laminated so that children can mark their progress with a dry-erase marker throughout the service. Children and families can then create their own worship bags filled with sensory items like fidgets, headphones, and sunglasses. These tools help individuals manage sensory overload and participate more comfortably in the service.

The sanctuary itself is equipped with sensory stations throughout, featuring foam blocks, coloring materials, and sensory bins. These stations are open for any child to use, regardless of diagnosis. "It's been great because we're not singling kids with autism out—other kids that use it, too," Stephanie notes.

Originally, Cross of Peace launched a separate sensory-friendly service, but post-COVID attendance realities made this unsustainable. Instead, they adapted their main service by shortening it to 40–45 minutes, replacing the passing of the peace with a non-contact gesture, and offering varied communion options to accommodate sensory needs and food allergies. They've even experimented with integrating therapy animals into worship.

The impact has been profound. Stephanie shares, "We have a few new families that have come who have no other outlets. It's just them and their kids all the time. For them to join a community that loves them and accepts their kids just as they are has been very fulfilling."

One of the most touching moments was a parents' night out event, where parents of children on the autism spectrum were able to enjoy a night out, many of them for the first time in a long time. They did it because they trusted the church to care for their children.

Despite challenges such as limited budget and Pastor Stephanie's bivocational role, Cross of Peace continues to expand its vision. They are now in the initial dreaming phases of developing an event space to provide employment opportunities for young adults on the autism spectrum.

Stephanie's vision for Cross of Peace is clear: "We now have a niche. We have a purpose." With a mission statement that reflects their commitment to inclusivity, Cross of Peace is truly welcoming all people across the spectrum.

Just a few miles away, another Minnesota congregation is extending that same spirit of welcome through a different format—by reimagining Vacation Bible School to meet the needs of children with sensory sensitivities.

Case Study #2 – Adaptive Vacation Bible School
Eden Prairie United Methodist Church (Eden Prairie, MN)

When Rachel Casper became Director of Children's Ministry at Eden Prairie United Methodist Church in 2019, she brought with her a par-

Chapter 3

ent's intuition and an advocate's heart. "I myself am an autism mom," she shared.

Her own son often couldn't participate fully in traditional children's ministry settings. During regular Vacation Bible School (VBS), for example, he would sit in the hallway during music time, overwhelmed by the crowd and noise. She had seen firsthand how limited options could quietly exclude children like him—not out of intention, but out of a lack of imagination and resources.

When in-person gatherings resumed after the pandemic, she approached her pastor with a vision for a sensory friendly VBS, and her pastor immediately said "yes," anchored in the Eden Prairie UMC's larger vision of welcome.

Adaptive VBS was born. Designed collaboratively by a core team of congregants with deep expertise, the program shifted the usual model. The team included a retired preschool teacher with experience working alongside autistic children, a retired occupational therapist, a special education teacher, a child psychologist, and a man who is himself on the spectrum.

Together, they reimagined the structure of VBS from the ground up. Children weren't grouped by age, but by needs—sensory seekers with sensory seekers, sensory avoiders with sensory avoiders. "We knew we needed to design a program where all of the kids could participate in all things," Rachel said. They also intentionally scheduled Adaptive VBS during the brief window between the end of summer school services and the start of the new academic year, when many families have limited support options.

In its first year, only four children participated, supported by a dozen volunteers. Since then, that number has hovered closer to 12 students for the last few years.

Every year brings new insights and God moments.

One child travels over ninety minutes and stays with his family in a hotel each summer just to be part of the week. Another child—a nonverbal participant—silent all week, suddenly joined the community in prayer on the final day by softly whispering, "Amen." "It made my year," Rachel shared.

The program schedule flexes with the needs of the children—no rigid time blocks, quiet rooms available at all times (they've learned they needed to add more), and parallel activities designed to honor every child's threshold for sensory processing. The presence of a gentle therapy dog—who also happens to have a disability—has become an annual highlight for all the children.

For many families, Adaptive VBS is their only point of connection to a faith community. And for the congregation, it has become a powerful reminder of Christ's call to welcome children—all children. "It's really opened our eyes," Rachel said. "We all know that people need food, or that people get sick. But I don't think everybody realized that there are kids who aren't always welcome in the church."

Adaptive VBS has helped create a space of delight for children and refuge for their caretakers. In this sacred space, children are free to be fully themselves, supported by volunteers who want to see them thrive.

Benefits and Challenges

When I consider this model of worship hospitality, the question isn't *if* we should do it, but *to what scale*. There are adults, children, and other young people in your congregation with sensory processing sensitivity. And if you do not have children in your congregation regularly, do not write this off: implementing some of these changes can be a great sign of welcome on Christmas and Easter, when visitors with children are more likely. Here are some of the benefits and challenges of implementing sensory sensitive worship practices in your congregation.

Benefits

- **Seeing is Caring** | When your church clearly names its commitment to sensory-sensitive worship, this allows those with sensory processing challenges to feel seen. For many, to feel seen is to feel known, and to feel known is to feel loved. By offering sensory-sensitive worship practices, we are providing

Chapter 3

opportunities for children to be known and loved by the church, but especially by Jesus.

- **Not Just for Children** | Sensory sensitive resources such as quiet rooms and self-regulating objects can be used by all generations.

- **Belong, Behave, Believe** | When children feel like they belong in worship, they will pick up on the common practices or behaviors of the church—the songs, the prayers, the teachings, the creeds, the sacraments, the community. Belonging leads to behaving and behaving leads to believing. To embrace sensory sensitive worship practices for children is to embrace a model of worship as formation and discipleship.

- **A Wealth of Products** | There are always new products and creative activities for those with sensory processing sensitivity. You can add or customize for your congregation and particular needs.

- **Deep Listening** | As a pastor or leader, you get the opportunity to listen to children and their families, working alongside them to identify needs and learn from them.

- **Pair it with a Pray-ground** | Pray-grounds and sensory sensitive worship practices are not mutually exclusive. While pray-grounds are located in the front of the church, they can still be supplied with sensory sensitive materials and activities.

Challenges

- **Getting it Wrong** | It's not enough to throw some sensory toys into a bin and declare that you are a sensory-sensitive congregation. Even with deep listening and intentional training, we can still get it wrong and be unintentionally inhospitable to particular families. Committing to being a sensory-sensitive community means committing to ongoing feedback and adjustments.

- **Highly Contextual** | There is no one-size-fits-all approach to sensory sensitivity in worship. While congregations such as Cross of Peace Lutheran Church may have focused more specifically on the autism community, not every church will have access to or the means to engage that community in meaningful ways.

- **Pushback** | Sometimes there might be naysayers who say things like, "we didn't have this (sensory sensitivity) in my day." The truth is, there have always been sensory sensitive people—we're just now more comfortable identifying it and talking about it. And thanks be to God that church can be a safe-enough place for people to be vulnerable in expressing their very-real and very-embodied concerns.

- **Specialized Volunteers** | Finding volunteers with personal or professional experience in sensory sensitivity can be challenging, and those who do have such experience may already be overextended. If specialized knowledge in sensory sensitivity is not apparent in your congregation, bringing in a subject matter expert to train a core group of volunteers is critical.

Next Steps

Implementing sensory sensitive worship practices for children involves four main processes, all of which may be overlapping: auditing, listening, building, and partnering.

Auditing your worship space and service(s) is a great first step. Pay attention to the various sensory experiences one might encounter, including the layout of the space, sounds, smells, lighting, and moments where there may be crowding of people or expected social interactions. Identify things that may be triggering and note suggestions for improvement.

At the same time, ensure you are *listening* to families of children with sensory sensitivities. To lead this listening process, find the people in your congregation who are passionate about this. It is best to have one designated leader or a small committee. Surveys, listening sessions, and one-on-one conversations can reveal both barriers to participation and opportunities for tailored approaches. This process ensures that any adjustments are shaped by real needs rather than assumptions. You don't have to only listen locally. Make an effort to interview churches in your geographic area, denomination, or network who are doing this well.

As you begin *building* your sensory sensitive ministry, starting small allows for gradual, meaningful progress. Begin with one or two simple adjustments, such as creating a quiet space near the sanctuary, offering sensory bags with fidget toys or noise-canceling headphones, or making changes to sound and lighting. Give at least a few months for these changes to settle in, solicit feedback, refine, and expand incrementally.

Finally, *partnering* with outside experts can strengthen your church's credibility in being a sensory sensitive community. Organizations like KultureCity offer certification processes, co-branding opportunities, training, and material resources. Consulting local schools, special education departments, or therapy centers is a great way to utilize subject matter experts and to offer training to your volunteers. These strategic partnerships can build connections with the wider community, positioning the church as a trusted ally.

Newly Calibrated Values

In the liturgy and the sacraments, we learn a new social imaginary, a new way of seeing the world, a new calibration of our values.

—Armond Léon van Ommen, *Autism and Worship*

I hope this chapter has invited us to reflect on the values of our worshiping communities. To what extent do our values and practices cater to "normal" worshipers with lesser regard to those who may be neurodivergent, autistic, and/or sensory sensitive?

In light of what we have learned about the gifts and challenges of sensory sensitive people, how might we newly calibrate those ecclesial values?

You may be wondering what any of this has to do with children *leading* in worship, and the answer is simple: everything. Being inclusive of sensory sensitive children in worship communicates that they belong and have a place in corporate worship. When sensory sensitive children engage worship on their own terms and at their own pace, this cultivates agency, which is intimately tied to leadership.

Taking steps toward a more sensory sensitive worship environment enriches the entire congregation. If our churches are spaces where all people—especially children—are seen, valued, and encouraged to lead, we are participating in the "already, but not yet" reality of God's Kingdom.

Resources to Engage

Visit abingdonpress.com/children-lead-extras for additional information and links to the following resources.

Archdiocese of Cincinnati – Belonging: Ministry with Persons with Disabilities
Resources for a sensory friendly Mass, which may inspire action in your own tradition.

KultureCity
The world's leading nonprofit on sensory accessibility and acceptance. The website includes training, resources, certifications, and projects to aid your congregation's implementation of sensory sensitive practices.

Autism Faith Network
A resource hub for faith communities seeking to better engage the autistic community.

Cross of Peace Lutheran Church
Check out their template for social scripts and visual cues for worship.

Worship Without Limits: Practical Guidance for Ministry Leaders Shepherding Individuals with Sensory Sensitivity
A fantastic research study and practical tools to better equip your congregation for sensory sensitive worship practices.

Chapter 4

Intergenerational Outreach

Not to overstate the obvious, but it is easy to observe that the Church is no longer at the center of society in the United States. Whether it's headlines about declining church membership, Sunday sports schedules, or memories of your own congregation's "glory days," it's clear the religious landscape has shifted. People are less religious than they once were, and folks are disaffiliating from belief at a much earlier age. According to the 2021 American National Family Life Survey, 26% of Americans who left their faith reported that this happened at age 12 or younger.

It is now more important than ever to engage children and their families. However, we cannot succumb to a "transactional" mindset of ministry where we build programs with the explicit outcome of institutional survival. The folks we want to bring into our buildings do not have a vested interest in institutional survival, and often for well-merited reasons. Trust in the institutional church is at an all-time low. "If you build it, they will come" no longer applies. How, then, do we engage children and families on their own terms, extending the Church to the neighborhoods, spaces, and places where families gather with children?

One movement invested in answering this question is Fresh Expressions. Originally based in the United Kingdom, the Fresh Expressions movement has expanded globally with a focus on innovative ways of being the Church. Some of this takes place within the walls of traditional institutions, while many fresh expressions take place in the community. The future of the Church is not to be found in strict organizational structures, but in a mixed ecology of embodying the communal, incarnational love of Jesus for the world.

There are four foundations of a fresh expression. It is *missional* in its effort to reach those who might not otherwise encounter a traditional church. It is *contextual* because it is often built around a mutual interest. It is *formational* in its explicit purpose of discipleship. And it is *ecclesial* insofar as this community of individuals function as a church for each other.

One of the most popular fresh expressions is the "dinner church," which is often intergenerational, centers upon a meal, storytelling, conversation, and prayer, while also including things like music, Holy Communion, or a missional focus. Other fresh expressions of the church may revolve around affinities such as running, gardening, video games, or service opportunities.

This chapter is not an advertisement for Fresh Expressions, but there is great wisdom in this movement. However, it is important to recognize that fresh expressions are more invested in the flourishing of the capital "C" Church than the numerical growth of the local church or denomination. As we explore some missional forms of engaging children in worship, we need to keep our intentions in check. Are we considering implementing these ministries just to grow our local church, or are we genuinely seeking out families, meeting them where they are, and introducing them to the love of God in Christ Jesus through worship?

For families with children who might not come to a Sunday morning worship service, there are other avenues where the church can meet families where they are and offer programs to nurture their agency and spiritual formation. This chapter will talk about two specific ways to do this: through programs like Messy Church and through arts-based programming such as children's theater. Churches that implement these programs may or may not be formally associated with the Fresh Expressions movement, but they are certainly offering a fresh expression of the Church for local families.

Messy Church

Messy Church emerged from St. Wilfrid's Church in Cowplain, UK, in 2004 as a creative response to the church's struggle to engage families with children. The church had beautiful facilities with a lot of creative volunteers, but few children in the congregation. They decided to create an intergenerational gathering where people could explore faith through hands-on, creative activities featuring storytelling, crafts, music, and shared meals. This "messy church" philosophy eventually became part of The Bible Reading Fellowship (BRF) in 2006 with the publication of the first *Messy Church* book by founder Lucy Moore. The movement has since expanded globally to a variety of denominations and traditions.

Messy Church is guided by five core values, which they explain in greater depth on their website (see Resources to Engage):

- Christ Centered: "Messy Church is a church, not a craft club, that helps people to encounter and enter into a transforming relationship with Jesus."

- All Ages: "Messy Church is for adults and children to enjoy together. Every element should be relevant and accessible to all ages."

- Creativity: "Messy Church uses hands-on activities to explore Bible stories, to reflect a God of creativity, and to give people a chance to play together."

- Celebration: "Messy Church reflects a God of joy who wants all of God's people to have life in all its fullness."

- Hospitality: "Messy Church reflects a God of unconditional love and is a church for people outside of a traditional church, providing an oasis of welcome and a safe place in which to thrive."

Churches have the flexibility to design a Messy Church experience in ways that match their priorities. The good news about the Messy Church

Chapter 4

network is that there is ample training, great resources, and a community of other churches and organizations also doing this work.

A typical Messy Church is broken down into four primary components: welcome, activities, celebration, and meal. Depending on the time of day the session is offered, these components can be moved around. With hospitality as a core value, Messy Church begins with a warm *welcome*. Then, all ages—children, siblings, friends, parents, grandparents, caretakers, volunteers—participate in *activities* and crafts that are centered upon a particular Bible passage or theme. The *celebration* component often includes interactive storytelling, music, and prayer. Finally, there is a *meal*. Each session involves food, cultivating community with friends old and new. If programming a particular session sounds overwhelming to you, Messy Church USA provides outlines and curricular resources to implement these sessions in your context.

I have seen firsthand the value of implementing a Messy Church program. When I served as pastor of Christ United Methodist Church in Neptune Beach, Florida, our ministry leadership team cast the vision for Messy Church, attended the trainings, and oversaw the launch of the program. Our aim was simple: build a bridge between the church and the 60 to 70 families associated with our preschool, not so that they could "join the church," but so that our distinct communities might interact in generative ways.

The program launch required many volunteers from the church and buy-in from the preschool directors, but it was a beautiful testimony to addressing a need that went unexpressed for a long time. Our preschool families rarely had opportunities to interact with one another as family units. Messy Church provided that opportunity at a convenient time (right after school pick-up) and in a well-known location (the church's fellowship hall, which was used for all major preschool events).

I remember receiving pushback against the word "Church" in Messy Church. Some felt like that word was too politically or psychologically loaded, while others felt like this would be a barrier to non-Christian participation. While the latter could be true, the goal of Messy Church is not to evangelize the nations. It's about showing folks that "church" can look a lot of different ways, and that even if you have a checkered history with the institutional church, you and your family are welcomed as full participants at Messy Church.

In the next case study, rather than highlighting a particular congregation, I sat down to chat with some of the national leaders of Messy Church USA to learn about their personal connections to the movement, some "best practices" for churches wanting to start this, and common pitfalls to avoid. We will also hear snippets of their testimonies of God's faithfulness through this movement.

Case Study #1 – Chatting with National Leaders
Messy Church USA

Messy Church USA has two fantastic leaders at its helm: Rev. Roberta Egli as Administrative Director and Dr. Johannah Myers as Program Director.

Both Roberta and Johannah came to Messy Church during seasons of transition, drawn by its ethos of relational, intergenerational worship. Roberta introduced it to her Oregon congregation and found it so life-giving that she eventually left traditional pastoral ministry to launch Messy Church USA. Johannah, likewise, was searching for a model that would serve entire families, not just children. Messy Church shifted her congregation's attention outward—toward schools, neighborhoods, and new community partnerships.

Their personal experiences in implementing Messy Church have shaped a clear vision of the conditions that help it thrive. Both emphasize the importance of attending official training sessions and connecting with the wider network for the sake of program longevity. "The churches that attend a training are much more apt to be doing Messy Church later," Roberta said.

Another best practice is being adaptable. "Your context is always going to be changing, so you have to be flexible," Roberta noted. Johannah recalled how simply relocating their gathering space to a room with round

Chapter 4

tables helped foster deeper relationships: "Everything felt calmer, more intentional. Relationships blossomed."

Team leadership is also essential. "It is not a ministry that should be done by one person," Johannah said. A team model "might not be the most efficient, but it is the most transformative." She encouraged leaders to see team development as discipleship: "Disciples are those who grow even as they help others grow."

A recurring pitfall, they warned, is reducing Messy Church to children's programming and losing sight of the intergenerational vision. The truth is that many adults want to have skin in the game and worship alongside their children. Johannah shared a formative moment when a parent said, "I'll go to an activity with my son, but I've never actually been invited to do the activity." At Messy Church, the hospitality of Christ is extended to all ages.

Impatience can also undermine the work, especially in churches that want quick results. Roberta cautioned against measuring success by numbers. "Messy Church is not a church growth movement," she said. "It's about building relationships that are long term."

Roberta and Johannah's testimonies highlight the relational nature of this ministry. Roberta recalled a grandfather who began bringing his grandsons to Messy Church. Initially disengaged, he opened up about being tired while raising these young boys due to his daughter's addiction. Over time, he found belonging and connection. "That's what I'm thinking about when I say that Messy Church is doing this *with* families rather than simply *for* them," Roberta said.

Johannah has seen similar stories of healing and welcome. Families who often feel alienated from typical Sunday worship services have found a home in their Messy Church. "We never set out to target anyone," she said. "But by doing Messy Church well, we created space for families to thrive." For those burned out by organized religion, Messy Church has become a lifeline for church exiles longing for intergenerational community.

"Messy Church"—the name itself holds a theologically poetic honesty. It's messy, not because it lacks structure but because it makes room for real life. And it's Church because everyone is welcomed in their mess and met by Love.

Worship and the Arts

Not long after I helped my congregation launch a Messy Church at the conclusion of 2022, I left parish-based pastoral ministry and followed God's calling to a university setting. I now serve as Director of the Center for Worship and the Arts at Samford University, whose mission is *equipping leaders of all ages for faithful and artistic worship through research, resources, and transformative gatherings—for the glory of God, for the good of the Church*. In this role, I have seen how young people connect to the worship of the Church so naturally through the arts. I've seen it in programs like Messy Church, and I've seen it in our flagship program Animate—a week-long intergenerational summer camp in worship and the arts. That said, in my current setting, most of these students are already a part of a local congregation. The greater challenge—and opportunity—is reaching those who are not.

Churches are uniquely positioned to reach families in the surrounding community as centers of teaching in the arts. Churches have physical space, volunteers or staff, connections with local musicians and artists, and—hopefully—a reputation of doing good in the community.

One common model for engaging children through outreach, especially among larger or well-resourced churches, is through a music academy. Several churches near me operate music academies that offer weekly lessons and culminate in some form of public performance, often within a worship context. These programs require significant coordination, but they can serve as vital outreach ministries, offering families affordable, high-quality music education while inviting them into the rhythms and relationships of church life.

If your church does not have the capacity to self-administer something like a music academy, consider partnering with an arts-based nonprofit. This could be through music, dance, visual art, theater, creative writing, or other artistic disciplines. Nonprofit arts organizations are often looking

Chapter 4

for affordable space in a convenient location. Churches can then support this nonprofit in other ways, such as by attending public performances, providing meals, or offering other points of connection for parents and caregivers while their children may be receiving instruction.

The case study that follows represents a hybrid of the academy and partnership models. We'll see how a small local church makes a big impact on its local community through a theater program.

Case Study #2 – Finding Nemo, and Finding Community for Children

Westover Hills United Methodist Church (Richmond, VA)

At Westover Hills United Methodist Church, a small suburban congregation in Richmond, Virginia, a thriving children's theater program has become an unlikely but powerful form of outreach and worship engagement. Led by Erin Thomas, Director of Administration and Creative Education, the program invites children from the surrounding community—not just the church—to participate in after-school musical productions like *Rudolph the Red-Nosed Reindeer*, *Frozen Jr.*, and *Finding Nemo Jr.*

Approximately 35 children are enrolled and meet weekly, with the program intentionally structured to do more than produce a show. "It's more important that they're here and they're safe, and they're having fun, and they feel supported," Erin explains. "It's just as important that we know their names, and they know each other's names, and they support one another at every given moment."

Each rehearsal ends with a shared meal and a time of guided conversation. Children are invited to reflect on their day with questions like: "Did you face a challenge today at school?" or "Was there a moment when you saw someone who needed help?" These moments of communal care and spiritual reflection are inspired by the church's current sermon series and other events.

Though the church averages 40–45 in Sunday worship and has few children in regular attendance, the theater program has become a point of connection with the broader community. Erin noted that several families involved in the program attended the church's Christmas Eve service. It wasn't planned. It simply happened as relationships formed and trust grew—an example of how the arts can gently open the door to a deeper sense of belonging.

Tuition is set at $275 for the semester—far lower than comparable Richmond programs—thanks to grant support from the United Methodist Foundation and the Virginia Conference. Scholarships are available to ensure access for all. Erin's dream is to expand the program into a bilingual format to serve immigrant families in the future.

The church community has embraced the program. "They show up for the show even though they don't have kids in it," Erin shared. "The night of the show here in the sanctuary, which seats over 350 people—you can't find a seat."

Erin sees God at work most clearly in the compassion the children show to one another. "When I see the younger ones instinctively supporting each other… that's what it is. It's: do all the good you can in all the ways you can. And those are the God moments."

Benefits and Challenges

When a church is intentional about reaching children in the wider community, it extends the hospitality of Christ, telling local families that they matter, regardless of their attendance on a Sunday morning. Outreach-based programming builds bridges that otherwise might not exist. Here are some benefits and challenges as you ponder ways of engaging children and families—whether beyond the church's walls or outside of traditional worship hours.

Benefits

- **Extending the Walls of the Church |** Not everyone feels comfortable in a church on Sunday mornings, but many long for connection with God and with others. Outreach-based programs allow churches to meet families in physical locations where they already feel comfortable, or with programs that are compelling and hospitable enough for them to step inside the church doors.

- **Low Start-Up Costs** | Initiatives like Messy Church or after-school arts programs can launch with minimal financial investment, especially when utilizing existing church space, materials, and volunteers. However, low start-up costs do not equate to low start-up effort!

- **Play to Your Strengths** | Each church has unique gifts—whether it's retired teachers, musicians, artists, or a well-used kitchen. Outreach programming allows congregations to tap into their specific strengths and passions for the benefit of the wider community.

- **Potential for Income Generation** | I feel like I'm not supposed to say this, but I'm going to say it anyway. Tuition-based arts programs or partnerships with nonprofits can provide modest income or offset costs, all while advancing the church's mission. We must not be afraid of these models, nor should we idolize them for revenue potential.

- **Renewed Sense of Purpose** | Many churches have become insular, focused only on Sunday morning worship, care of members, and sustaining existing programs for the sake of nostalgia or lack of vision clarity. Outreach programs can reinvigorate a congregation's sense of mission and remind members why the Church exists in the first place.

Challenges

- **Impact Hard to Measure** | Outreach-based ministries often yield long-term relationships and broader community recognition. In our culture of immediacy, these programs may not seem to yield fruit by our usual measurements. Success must be redefined in terms of the cultivation of trust, wider networks, and community stakeholders who may not be associated with your church.

- **Sufficient Volunteers** | Many churches already feel stretched for help. Sustaining these outreach efforts requires committed and trained volunteers who see this as ministry, not just programming.

- **Keeping Discipleship at the Core** | Sometimes outreach-based models can be so heavily programmed that the church may feel pressure to minimize its spiritual role. Resist that urge, and serve this outreach-based ministry to the best of your ability. Embody the hospitality of Christ. To all who interact with your programming, offer on-ramps and points of connection to a life of faith.

Next Steps

There is no singular solution for how best to engage children and families in worship through outreach-based models. By assembling a small team and working through the following questions with prayerful discernment, you will be on the right track.

What are the real needs of children and families in our community? If you haven't already consulted a data service like MissionInsite, it can be a helpful tool for understanding the demographic and socioeconomic complexities of your area. Beyond data, talk to people. Connect with school principals, aftercare coordinators, social workers, or local nonprofit leaders who work with families every day.

What gifts and assets has God already placed within your congregation? If you have not done any asset mapping of your congregation, this is a great way to identify the resources of your physical property, the gifts and talents of your congregation members (including artistic ones), and the relevant points of connection with stakeholders and organizations in your wider community. God has likely already provided what you need to begin.

What is motivating this effort? Are you hoping to grow your church, or are you genuinely seeking to love the children and families who are your neighbors? Be honest. If your goal is simply to double your children's ministry in two years, it may be time to reconsider and reframe.

What existing relationships or potential partnerships could support this work? No congregation does this work alone. Could you partner with a local arts organization, or even another local church? How can responsibility be shared and resources used wisely? Collaboration can increase the capacity and credibility of your own church, too.

Who is missing from the table as we discern these next steps? Look around the room. If you are trying to serve children and families, are there any young families with children who are on your team? Or if your church was trying to launch a Vacation Bible School for Spanish-speaking children, but did not include any native speakers on the team, this would be a red flag. Let the makeup of your team reflect the mission itself.

How will spiritual formation and discipleship remain at the center? As the team makes plans, consider how families with children may be led in prayer, reflection, storytelling, and other faith practices that reflect Christ.

What are you willing to let go of in order to try something new? Perhaps there are other programs, traditions, or expectations that need to be released in order to create space for this new work.

Perhaps most relevant to this book: What is the connection to worship? What is the link between this outreach and your church's worshiping life? Can children's voices, stories, or creative gifts be brought into worship? Are there ways your program itself becomes a form of worship—through prayer, music, or shared meals?

Once you have discerned and prayed together, the answers to these questions will help shape a strategic plan guided by the Holy Spirit. While outreach-based models of engaging children and families do not always seem the most logical, efficient, or even convenient, that is exactly the kind of soil in which the Kingdom of God tends to germinate and grow—thanks be to God.

Serve Your Context

The local church may no longer be at the center of society, but that does not mean it has lost its calling to reflect the love of Christ to children and families. Instead, the church is invited to think more creatively about how it presents itself to its surrounding community.

In the realm of worship, the Church has a strong trajectory of taking its local community seriously and adapting its practices to reflect the surrounding context. We call this *liturgical inculturation*, which is a biblically rooted, historically informed, and Spirit-led process of allowing worship to take on the language, symbols, and practices of a local people, without losing the heart of the gospel.

Messy Church is a liturgy that feels familiar to children and families, even if it's not the Sunday morning worship experience. It embodies the heart of liturgical inculturation, honoring the patterns of family life—shared meals, creativity, playfulness, and storytelling—and weaving them into a worshipful framework where Christ is at the center.

Likewise, arts-based outreach programs equip children with tangible skills: singing, acting, playing an instrument, creating visual art, or dancing. These gifts offer children ways to express themselves, grow in confidence, and perhaps one day shape how they participate in the worship life of the Church—even if that connection feels tangential or unformed right now.

Taken together, these outreach-based models—and the case studies that support them—expand our imagination of what worship is and who is being formed to lead it. Therefore, go forth and seek new ways of embodying Christ's love to children and families in your community. Map your assets. Engage the arts. Recalibrate your expectations of success. And plant seeds—not for quick results, but for Kingdom flourishing.

Resources to Engage

Visit abingdonpress.com/children-lead-extras for additional information and links to the following resources.

Chapter 4

Fresh Expressions USA
Important information about Fresh Expressions USA, and trainings and resources for how your church can be involved.

Messy Church USA
The central hub for all Messy Church USA information and operations. This website includes important training opportunities, resources both free and paid, and opportunities for membership and networking.

The Quick and Simple Congregational Asset-Mapping Experience
Produced by the Alban Institute, this great resource will walk your congregation through the process of asset mapping.

MissionInsite
Demographic analysis to fuel your church's missional impulse. Generate a detailed report about the people in your community, which may reveal strategies about how to better engage them.

Chapter 5
Church-School Partnerships

At the time of writing, my daughter is four years old and attends a non-religiously-affiliated preschool that—to me—has an unclear relationship with the local Presbyterian church that leases space to them. Many of the preschool activities take place in the fellowship hall of the church, I have attended parent-teacher conferences in the church's library, and there are often strategically placed posters for family-oriented events sponsored by the church. However, at any of the school-wide events, I've never met a single church member, church staff member, or the pastor.

While there may be logical reasons for this of which I am unaware, I find it both odd and a missed opportunity. Meanwhile, even though her school does not have a Christian faith component, I have experienced many public prayers from school leaders addressed to Jesus, as well as my child learning prayers in the classroom. Very likely this is a product of our family living in the US Deep South, but nonetheless, I wish the local church were more present in matters of faith.

Across the United States there are many early childhood education programs that have a connection to a church. According to the 2019 National Survey of Early Care and Education (NSECE), there are approximately 7,550 centers sponsored by a church or a religious private school, serving 432,000 children and representing 6.2% of centers. Additionally, there are 14,700 centers located in faith-based buildings but not sponsored by a church or religious private school, serving 853,000 children and representing 12.1% of centers. The remaining 98,800 centers are neither sponsored by a church or religious private school nor located in buildings associated with faith-based organizations, serving 5.87 million children and representing 81.7% of centers.

While it's clear that religiously-affiliated early education centers are in the minority—either by sponsorship or by their physical space—it still represents a combined 18.3% of centers and 1.2 million children being served. In other words, partnership opportunities abound. If your church has a relationship with a preschool, this chapter is for you.

Even if your church is not connected with a preschool, opportunities also abound with elementary schools, private and public. While public school partnerships can be more complex, the challenges are not insurmountable. If your church is partnered with a local school or wants to build a partnership, this chapter is also for you.

Church-Preschool Partnerships

Many churches have relationships with preschools. Sometimes the preschool is an active ministry of the church with strong overlapping staff and a lot of crossover between preschool families and church members. In other circumstances, it may be set up as a separate organization with its own staffing, yet still maintain a connection—even if in name only—with the local congregation. And based on the NSECE survey mentioned earlier, the most common association is a landlord-tenant relationship. The information in this chapter will be more directly relevant to the first two scenarios but may also apply to healthy and cooperative landlord-tenant situations.

Church-preschool partnerships are characterized by, at minimum a worship service or religious education. Over and above this are things like joint events, arts and music education, and a preschool leadership board with varying degrees of church oversight. Your church may be doing some or all of this, or even more.

In speaking with pastors and leaders, and in my own ministry experience with churches that have preschools, I have found two common dynamics in these partnerships. The first is on the church side, where the average congregant wishes the preschool were more connected to the local church. Often this is rooted in a transactional mindset (get the children in, grow the church), but sometimes it is also rooted in nostalgia for when the church and preschool were once better integrated. Interestingly, although a desire for a stronger connection is there, sometimes church members think it's the preschool's job or the pastor's job to make this happen.

The other dynamic is the preschool that may—for good reasons—not want the church to be too involved. Faith-based early childhood educators often understand an important reality that seems to soar past the average churchgoer: families have many reasons for choosing a childcare facility that have little to with the sponsoring church. It could be location, cost, hours of operation, cleanliness, licensure of staff, number of meals or snacks provided, or just the plain fact that there are openings in a competitive market! Sometimes preschool directors try to keep church members at arm's length, especially those who are overzealous in recruiting preschool families to attend their Sunday morning services.

Even though the selection of a preschool often has little to do with the denomination or the church itself, this doesn't mean the faith commitments of the associated facility are insignificant. In the 2021 report, "Examining the Role of Faith-Based Childcare," by the Bipartisan Policy Center, they offer some statistically significant reasons for why parents choose faith-based centers over others:

- 32% of parents in a faith-based center report *approaches to cognitive development* as a top factor, compared to 24% of parents in non-faith-based centers.

- 25% of parents in a faith-based center in January 2020 selected *individualized attention to their child*, compared to 17% in non-faith-based centers.

- 29% of parents in a faith-based center in January 2020 selected *approaches to social-emotional learning*, compared to 16% in non-faith-based centers.

Chapter 5

Cognitive development, individualized attention, and a faith-based center's approach to social-emotional learning—all of these point to a common dynamic: faith-based centers especially care about forming the *whole person*.

Faith formation is caring for the whole person, and church leaders can steward that well. For churches with preschools, we may not have a lot of overlap in membership or attendance between the preschool and the church, but we do have the gift of children right in our backyards. By committing ourselves to working toward a successful partnership, children can be formed as whole persons, can be discipled, and can have opportunities to lead in worship. The following case study is a great example of a church-preschool partnership that is healthy, but with plenty of growing edges.

Case Study #1 – Strengthening Partnership through Worship
First United Methodist Church (Sarasota, FL)

In downtown Sarasota, First United Methodist Church is a vibrant worshiping community with a highly regarded preschool serving nearly 70 children, from infants to VPK (Voluntary Prekindergarten). "We're one of the few downtown options for preschool for parents who work downtown," explains Laura Ross, Kids and Youth Ministry Director. Laura was brought on staff to strengthen family ministries and build deeper connections between the church and preschool.

Two features of this partnership relate directly to worship. The first is the music program, where the church's music minister leads preschool children in age-appropriate choral music. At periodic points in the year, the preschool children who participate are invited to lead on Sunday mornings in front of the congregation, regardless of whether or not the children are associated with the church.

The second worship-related feature are the chapel sessions, which Laura leads and are held on Tuesday mornings for the oldest preschool groups—3s, 4s, and 5s. With about 25 students in her care and classroom teachers also in attendance, Laura leads these sessions using the Godly Play curriculum. Laura describes a typical chapel session: "We do candle lighting, our scripture story in the Godly Play style, a song, and then we pray together." She often teaches the same lesson on Sunday mornings, providing consistency and helping children forge connections between weekday chapel and church worship.

When asked to share a "God-moment" from the church-preschool partnership, Laura recalled a recent experience during Lent. As the preschoolers rehearsed for their Palm Sunday song in the sanctuary, they noticed the cross had been lowered and draped in purple. Without prompting, they began explaining its meaning: that purple is important, rare, and reminds us that God is coming as a king. Laura was deeply moved to hear them echo the very language she uses in chapel worship services and how these children really "get it."

Beyond chapel and music, Laura is intentional about building relationships with preschool families. She regularly attends school events like parent snack times and "Donuts with Grownups," so that parents can put a face to the person their kids talk about when they mention chapel. The church also invites preschool families to participate in church events, with some success. They have found that consistency is key, even if engagement is lower than expected.

Of course, the work is ongoing. Laura acknowledges that the partnership is still growing and that not all church members are fully aware of the preschool's role. "Some people are very aware of it, while others don't realize that we have a preschool until the kids show up on Sunday morning to sing," she says.

The partnership between First United Methodist Church of Sarasota and its preschool is both a testimony to God's love and a work in progress—one that offers a replicable model for how churches can break down walls between the congregation and the preschool to nurture the youngest in their care.

Chapter 5

Church-Elementary School Partnerships

In the public school arena, most church-school partnerships are based on missional needs. Churches are doing the excellent and needed work of summer lunch assistance, providing clothes, stocking food pantries and school supply closets, offering tutoring, and more. While the separation of church and state will not allow churches to do anything that would directly involve children in the leadership of worship, there are still other opportunities for engagement.

Even the word "partnership" is tricky and may only be appropriate language from the church's "side" of the partnership. In most circumstances, there cannot be any formal agreement, and the church must enter into the collaboration with humility, recognizing the school's priorities and constraints. Two common ways churches connect with local elementary schools are by offering after-school programs or sponsoring clubs and activities on campus.

Off-site after-school care programs are administratively easier to handle, but more difficult to get children to attend. This works best when the church is located near the school, already has relationships with students, and can offer transportation or incentives that make participation easier for families. In these programs, churches often provide time and space for students to finish their homework and may supplement that with tutoring, snacks, recreation, or arts education. Music or arts education is one of the most natural connections churches can make with worship.

Conversely, sponsored clubs and activities require far more diplomacy and administrative prowess, but may be easier for children to attend. For these to work, you will need—at minimum—a few "anchor" students and at least one teacher or school administrator to sponsor the club or activity. The church would not be the official sponsor of the club, but it could come alongside the students and teachers in facilitating the club. Bible clubs are common, which may include worship and prayer components. Alternatively, if you had the right personnel, you could start a children's choir that sings sacred music, launch a dance troupe, or lead something like an audio-visual technology club. All these art forms have natural bridges to the worship life of the church. That said, unless you have a long-term plan and sustained volunteer leadership, it may be more practical to focus your energy on an off-site program hosted by the church.

The next case study models what a healthy after school program can look like through musical instruction.

Case Study #2 – After School Music Education
Sound Space (Trinity United Methodist Church, Colusa, CA)

In Colusa, California—a 6,000-person town where nearly 50% of the population is immigrant, mostly from Mexico and other Latino/a/e nationalities—Trinity United Methodist Church has become a vital community space for local children. The church's after-school music program, *Sound Space*, offers children creative outlets and a safe [and "sound"] space to explore music, guided by lay leader Elizabeth Yerxa and her team.

Sound Space was created to serve an immediate need. Elizabeth explains, "We have a wonderful elementary school music teacher here in Colusa . . . but the school district lost the other music educators for older students for a couple of years, so there was no music at the 4th through 12th-grade level at that time." Recognizing the church's own talent pool and other creatives in the community, Elizabeth's pastor and church leaders saw an opportunity for the church to step in.

Structured as a separate entity, *Sound Space* is a nonsectarian program with no religious content. It is intentionally designed that way so it can partner officially with the public school system and others, such as the city, local theater, and the area arts council. The program serves 4th to 6th graders and offers a variety of activities like hand chimes, folk songs, singing for musical theater, and ukulele lessons. Lessons are structured for six weeks, usually followed by a concert open to the public. Registration is subsidized by grant funding, and many students receive scholarships based on financial need.

Elizabeth credits the community's support for the program's success: "It was really not nearly as hard as I thought it was going to be to draw children in for an after-school program." There's also buy-in from the high school, where students help by walking children to the church and by serving as volunteers, creating connections across generations and satisfying the need for highly coveted service hours.

While music is at the core of *Sound Space*, its broader mission is to offer children a place where they feel welcome and supported. Elizabeth notes, "A lot of the kids that we have may never join this church, but it may be the only connection they have to a church." This reflects a vision of arts-based ministry that extends beyond Sunday mornings.

While *Sound Space* was designed primarily to serve the community, there has been a trickle effect into other parts of church life. Elizabeth shares, "A lot of the people who have come to *Sound Space* are now coming back for other things." This includes attendance at the church's contemplative service, "Mid-Month Mondays," where people gather for a quiet, meditative time.

Regular church members are very supportive of the program. They participate by attending concerts, helping with snacks, and supporting the upkeep of the *Sound Space* room. The quilting team even created beautiful sound-dampening quilts to adorn the space.

Through *Sound Space*, Trinity United Methodist Church demonstrates a new approach to ministry. Elizabeth challenges the idea that church involvement should only be about filling pews on Sundays. In this way, *Sound Space* is not merely a musical program; it is a ministry that redefines what it means to be a community-centered church in a small town.

The *Sound Space* program is an excellent example of how a church can create lasting connections for children through a shared love of music and the arts. And even though Jesus is not named in this programming, he's certainly at work through it!

Benefits and Challenges

Whether you are contemplating ways to strengthen an existing church-school partnership or considering ideas for a new one, here are some benefits and challenges that may help your discernment.

Benefits

- **Creative Resource Sharing** | Your church likely has unused space during the week—use it to support an after-school program! You also likely have unused musical instruments, audio visual technology, and craft supplies that could be put to good use. Additionally, there are creative folks in your congregation looking for ways to serve. This can work to your benefit for any type of school-based partnership.

- **Being Niche** | Do you have church members who are passionate about a particular art form that can connect with worship? For example, imagine you have some talented photographers in your church. What if you started a photography after-school program that met once per week? What if the photographs taken were relevant to the worship series at hand and used in the Sunday morning worship service? What if you invited the children and their families to worship so they could see their photos in action, or hosted an art exhibit once per semester, showing their work?

- **Intergenerational Opportunities** | Especially for preschool programming, which often takes place in the middle of a workday, older congregants—many of whom may be retired—can offer their time and talents to support programming.

- **People Feel Valued** | When I pastor churches, one question I often ask leadership teams is "If we were to cease to exist today, who in the community would be mourning our loss?" Church-school partnerships are relational investments that help families with children feel valued. Theologically, we know that people are loved and valued by God—and programs like these make it feel even more tangible.

Challenges

- **Getting Our Hopes Up** | For church pastors, leaders, and attendees, it's easy to get our hopes up thinking that these programs will lead to young families attending our churches. No matter how good our intentions are about not being "transactional" in our thinking, the hope is always there. For any church-school partnership, we should expect to give—of our time and resources—without wanting anything in return. This mindset requires intentional teaching so that church members can see the Kingdom value in an investment that may seem "one-sided."

- **Responsibility Deferral** | Everyone shares responsibility in making a partnership work. Guard against it being one-sided through clear leadership structures, communication plans, regular check-ins, and year-end evaluations.

- **Finding Connections to Worship** | This will involve creativity and strategic planning, as many of the students—whether preschool or elementary—may not have a strong connection to your local church. As such, it is best to temper expectations about any kind of regular worship attendance or leadership in worship. While we do want children to lead, we have to balance that with the potential competing priorities of their parents and caregivers.

- **Volunteer Capacity** | In US-based church culture, many people are fine with Sunday commitments, but participating, much less leading, during weekdays can be challenging. Prior to strategizing about your church-school partnership, you will need a deep bench of volunteers to sustain any kind of future programming.

Next Steps

To form a new church-school partnership or to strengthen an existing one, discern your church's role. No congregation can do everything—and that's not the goal. The goal is to listen deeply, and respond in ways that are both faithful to your community and sustainable. Consider these questions for communal discernment:

- What is our congregation uniquely gifted to offer?
- Where is the Spirit already at work in our neighborhood and school?
- Who in our church already has meaningful connections with the school?
- What do we have the capacity to do consistently, even if we start small?

Discernment invites you to think not only about what your church can give, but also how your church might grow through mutual relationship.

If you do not already have a good relationship with school leadership, seek out opportunities to build one. Once you have developed that relationship, ask important questions. In Jake McGlothin's book, *The Mission-Minded Guide to Church and School Partnerships*, he shares a story about his senior pastor who approached the school principal and asked, "What keeps you up at night?" This simple question and the principal's honest response led to a powerful partnership that continues today, over fifteen years later.

As it relates to equipping children with skills that may help with leadership in worship, consider asking your school leaders questions like:

- Where do you see leadership emerging in your students, and how can we help nurture it?
- What kinds of creative expression do your students enjoy most—music, storytelling, movement, visual art?

- Are there opportunities for us to support you in creating spaces where children feel seen, heard, and valued?
- How might we collaborate to help children tell their own stories in ways that build confidence and community?

At the same time, your church will want to show that it is invested in other ways. School leaders are quick to sniff out relationships that seem one-sided. Make sure there is a church presence in areas of volunteering, attending or sponsoring school-related functions, and participating in the parent-teacher association, if applicable. However, it's not only about the church serving the school. Identify key leaders from the school to speak on topics they are passionate about. Plug them into Sunday morning worship, at relevant events, or during various leadership team meetings.

As you are identifying ways to partner, form your team to think through the nuts and bolts of the programming. Aim to start small and manageable.

For preschool partnerships, your church has a rich opportunity to teach young ones through worship. If you can aim for a weekly chapel service, that is preferable because the predictability will also help the curricular rhythms on the preschool side. You don't need to overthink the lessons or be an "expert" in theology or early childhood education. For some of the students in your care, this may be the only time they experience the central stories of the Christian faith. Teach them the gospel: from creation, to crisis, to covenant, to the Church, to Christ, to the new creation. Sing with them, even if you're not a polished singer. Teach them simple, memorable, timeless songs. Anything you do above and beyond this is icing on the proverbial cake!

For elementary school partnerships, if you are leaning toward an after-school program, consider the value of a daily program versus a weekly program. A daily after school program will require far more administration with appropriate staffing. However, you may be able to offset costs by charging tuition on a sliding scale or securing grant funding for scholarships or subsidization. If you are considering a weekly rhythm, make it a free program of the church, and even consider arranging transportation, provided it's in harmony with the school system policies.

In general, revenue-based models of programming can be tricky. While additional income can be helpful, the clearest witness of your partnership will be how freely and generously it offers hospitality to children and families.

Faithfulness for the Long-Haul

In all that we do by way of partnership, we also need to be realistic: children won't start flooding our sanctuaries just because we offer compelling music education or host a chapel service. And that's okay. We may see some families or school staff take interest in our church community over time—but those instances may be few and far between. Church-school partnerships are about faithfulness for the long-haul.

That said, even when the connection to corporate worship is tenuous, it's still a connection. A chapel song remembered, a Sunday morning opportunity of leadership, a photograph displayed in worship, a parent who learns something about God from their 4-year-old child—all these moments are touchpoints of grace.

Church-preschool partnerships are ripe with possibility. And it's not one person's "job" to make this happen: everyone shares responsibility. When we show up consistently, listen closely, and love generously, we create space for God to move in ways we might not expect. And over time, that quiet faithfulness becomes a witness in the lives of children, families, and congregations alike.

Resources to Engage

Visit abingdonpress.com/children-lead-extras for additional information and links to the following resources.

Jake Mcglothin. *The Mission-Minded Guide to Church and School Partnerships.* Abingdon Press, 2017.

Chapter 5

Partnering your church family with a public school can be a rewarding experience, but it also presents some unique challenges. This book offers practical steps congregations can take to make a difference with the children in their community.

2019 NSECE Snapshot: The Role of Faith-based Organizations in Center-based Child Care and Early Education
This snapshot presents estimates of the role of faith-based organization in center-based CCEE (Child Care and Early Education) using data from the 2019 NSECE (National Survey of Early Care and Education).

Bipartisan Policy Center, "Examining the Role of Faith-Based Child Care," 2021 Report.
This report helps us know why parents and caregivers select faith-based child care over other options.

Sound Space
Here you can read about the programming of Sound Space, a program of Trinity United Methodist Church in Colusa, California.

Chapter 6
Children in Contemporary Worship

Depending on how you chronicle history, the "contemporary worship" movement is old enough that it will soon be eligible to apply for Medicare. In the most basic linguistic sense, contemporary worship is worship that is "with the times" (*con* "with" and *tempus* "time"). Over the latter half of the twentieth century, we have come to equate contemporary worship with band-centric popular musical forms, the use non-archaic English in liturgical speech and song lyrics, and informal styles of leadership.

In Lester Ruth and Swee Hong Lim's book *A History of Contemporary Praise and Worship*, they argue for two distinct historical "rivers" of this movement: praise and worship, emerging primarily from Pentecostal and charismatic movements, and contemporary worship, emerging from Mainline Protestantism and classic Evangelical denominations. The praise and worship river understands these musical forms to be a gift through which the presence of God is made manifest. A scriptural paradigm for this is Psalm 22:3, where God "inhabits" or is "enthroned" on "the praises" of God's people Israel. The contemporary worship river understands these musical forms to be a pragmatic tool to win people to Christ, attract young people, and fill the pews. The scriptural anchor for this river is Paul's declaration in 1 Corinthians 9 to be "all things to all people" so that some may be saved. It is also worth noting that the praise and worship river was more racially and ethnically diverse, while the contemporary worship river was predominantly white.

In the 1980s, these musical forms were often led by a "worship leader," which was a new title and an upgrade in leadership responsibilities compared to the "song leader" of decades prior. The 1980s and 1990s also observed the rise of the megachurch, often with these contemporary worship forms front and center. Around the same time, Christian radio became increasingly popular in disseminating this music, with many of these songwriters and worship leaders attaining near-celebrity status depending on the audience.

These new musical forms, new liturgical leadership, and new modes of being the church all coalesced in the 1990s and early 2000s. Concurrently, these two rivers of praise and worship and contemporary worship, once rather distinct, now formed a kind of floodplain where they became harder to distinguish. Ruth and Lim create the term "contemporary praise and worship" as a catch-all moniker to recognize the cross-pollinated nature of these histories.

Fast forwarding to today, contemporary praise and worship is ubiquitous across denominations. It is also commonly described as a style of music or worship that attracts "young people," even though church attendance data tells a different story. However, even if it is true that young people *prefer* contemporary worship music over other forms (the jury is still out, I think) one important question remains: Why are there so few children and other young people involved in the *leadership* of contemporary worship?

Contemporary Worship Music with Children

Prior to serving as an ordained pastor, I served as a contemporary worship leader for a variety of churches and denominations. This was not a style of worship that I tried to adopt—my home church formed me in it. While it was a United Methodist congregation, we had no hymnals, nor did I ever flip through *any* hymnal with intentionality until I went to seminary.

In all my years of leading worship, I never considered incorporating children in worship. That might sound like a disqualifier for writing this chapter—but I think the opposite is true. I've come to understand what held me back, and I know what I would do differently if I could go back in time. When we ask, "Why are there so few children and other young people involved in the *leadership* of contemporary worship?" so much of this boils down to one word: *excellence*.

A simple Google search about worship and excellence will reveal a myriad of scripture-backed insights for why things like professionalism and good musicianship are critical to successful contemporary worship. Psalm 33 exhorts musicians to play "skillfully." The construction of the Temple in 1 Kings and 2 Chronicles was also an act of worship done with utmost professionalism. The line of thinking is that we offer our excellence because God's very nature is excellent, and God deserves our best.

In practice, excellence becomes a barrier for the participation of many in contemporary worship services. And it's not only musical barriers. Services that offer contemporary worship have also been taught to value good "flow" in worship. This often translates to people with refined oratorical skills leading most of the service. Good music and good flow require a level of professionalism in audio, visual, and lighting support.

From the perspective of many, children are obstacles to excellence. They may not sing the right notes or come in at the right time in the song. They may get distracted or even be a distraction to others on the platform. Children require more time and effort in rehearsals, all of which may detract from the excellence of the overall service. While many of these things may be true (although let's not pretend that all adults are perfect exemplars), I think we are missing the larger point.

When we exclude an entire generation of worshipers from leadership, worship is no longer "the work of the people"—it's the work of professionals.

I'm convinced that God does not care as much about our excellence as much as God cares about our faithfulness. In 1 Corinthians 1, we read

Chapter 6

that we have been "enriched" in Christ "in every way" and are not lacking in any spiritual gift as we await the coming of Christ among us. We are called to be faithful and to "keep firm" in using the gifts that God has given us. In worship services, faithfulness means giving our best, even if that "best" does not meet worldly standards of professionalism. Faithfulness means honoring excellence without idolizing it. And faithfulness in worship involves multiple generations, especially children.

Children can lead in diverse ways in contemporary worship. It's not a matter of handing them a microphone and letting them sing with the ensemble. They can be greeters or ushers. They can lead from the pews in helping their parents give an offering. They can sing in a choir—age segmented or intergenerational. They can read scripture. They can lead the Lord's Prayer. They can dance. They can testify. And yes, they can preach. So, let's encourage their leadership and see how our faithfulness meets God's.

To explore what this kind of faithfulness can look like in practice, let's turn to two churches that are actively empowering children to lead in contemporary worship settings.

Case Study #1 – Worship Shaped by Children
Hutchinson Missionary Baptist Church (Montgomery, AL)

Hutchinson Missionary Baptist Church in Montgomery, Alabama, is a majority-African American congregation of approximately 260-300 worshipers each Sunday, including around 35 children. Their worship style embraces a mix contemporary gospel music and more traditional components—all energetic, vibrant, and reflective of the congregation's priorities. Yet the most distinctive aspect of Hutchinson is their intentional integration of children and teens into the regular planning and leading of worship.

Rather than limiting youth participation to an annual "Youth Sunday," Hutchinson includes young people as consistent, active worship leaders. Pastor Cameron Thomas explains, "We have a Youth Sunday every month. Our children are leading worship regularly, which allows them to grow into their leadership roles." This monthly rhythm normalizes children's presence and does not reduce their contributions to something novel or for entertainment purposes.

Planning for these worship services is equally distinctive. Children and teens participate alongside adults in weekly worship planning meetings, directly shaping the content and direction of the services. They contribute ideas about scripture passages, song selections, and artistic elements, provide feedback, and engage in theological reflection about worship. This practice builds on a long-standing tradition within Black churches of affirming children's presence and gifts in worship, while also pushing that tradition further—toward a model of sustained and structured leadership. As Pastor Thomas puts it, the goal is not to showcase children as performers but to empower them as genuine theological leaders: "It's all about providing space for youth and children to see their essential role in the Sunday morning worship experience."

Initially, some adults in the congregation expressed skepticism, worried that giving children so much agency would result in disorder or superficiality. However, these fears dissipated over time as congregants witnessed the depth and theological maturity young leaders brought to worship. The model has helped create a culture of mutual learning, where children are not only being shaped by their elders, but also shaping the faith of the adults around them. When children's roles in planning and leadership are normalized, the whole community benefits.

Pastor Thomas reflects on this beautifully: "When we give space for our children to lead, we are not only shaping their future but enhancing our worship today." At Hutchinson Missionary Baptist Church, children lead because they have something essential and faithful to offer. Their voices matter—to the church, and to God.

In making room for children to lead, Hutchinson has not only elevated their voices, but also rediscovered its own.

Case Study #2 – Growing Worship Leaders at All Stages
Hosanna! Lutheran Church (St. Charles, IL)

At Hosanna! Lutheran Church in St. Charles, Illinois—a congregation affiliated with Lutheran Congregations in Mission for Christ (LCMC)—

Chapter 6

Dr. Melody Kuphal has been building a culture of intergenerational worship leadership for over a decade. Rooted in her conviction that "kids are equipped to lead worship at every age," Melody regularly programs young ones to lead in corporate worship.

One of the core programs at Hosanna! is a Tuesday evening music ministry that gathers over 70 children from a range of local churches. After open gym time, kids join age-tiered choir rehearsals and musical instruction. A highlight for elementary students is the original songwriting process that begins each January. Working within the theme of that year's Vacation Bible School (VBS), the kids help write a song from scratch—and sometimes even choreograph a line dance—learning both creativity and collaboration along the way.

Alongside writing original music, Melody and her praise team of older elementary schoolers also adapt existing worship songs to make them age appropriate. Many are drawn from CCLI catalogs, but they're rarely used as-is. "We're editing songs down to about two minutes," she said, "but still honoring the original intent." Keys are adjusted to suit young voices, elements and repetition are narrowed, and the overall goal is clarity, singability, and closeness to scripture. This praise team is distinct from Hosanna's Sunday morning band, which youth may join after completing 7th grade. And even after those students graduate and head off to college, Melody makes sure they're scheduled to play and sing when they're home—reinforcing that their gifts still matter and that they remain a valued part of the worshiping community.

On Sunday mornings, children are regularly visible and active in worship. The children's choir leads worship monthly at Hosanna's contemporary service, which is often attended by families with children due to its timing and typically draws between 150–200 worshipers, about 50 of whom are children. These leadership opportunities include singing, reading Scripture, and even composing call-and-response elements tailored for early readers. As Melody notes, "We think long and hard about any call and response that has words longer than six letters. . . . The word Hallelujah is longer, but some words are worth learning." The emphasis is always on age-appropriate empowerment.

Melody is the first to admit that forming kids as worship leaders takes time and is not particularly efficient. But the result is a culture where children know they belong, and more importantly, where they know they're needed. Whether it's shouting "He's coming!" on Palm Sunday, offering original artwork during the sermon as their offering to be shared with shut-ins, or belting out the Apostles' Creed louder than the grown-ups, these children are not waiting to be invited into worship. They already belong there, and they are leading.

Benefits and Challenges

In both case studies, we see the efforts these two congregations make to regularly incorporate children into the leadership of worship. These are not simple adjustments, but significant alterations to the culture of their congregations. If you are interested in making this change in your context, consider the following benefits and challenges.

Benefits

- **Leadership Incubator** | When you create a steady volunteer base of children, you are making an investment in their leadership. Through leading on Sunday mornings, children are offered a sense of ownership and responsibility to grow in their gifts. This investment in young leaders ripples out to parents, who become more committed to their children's spiritual growth and can actively support their development at home.

- **Intentional Teaching during Planning** | If you take cues from Hutchinson Missionary Baptist Church, children who are helping to plan worship will both learn a lot and teach us things about worship. For example, while children may learn important information about the liturgical year and which songs fit with certain scriptures, they will also teach us about what other children value in worship, and even more deeply, they will teach us about the character of God.

Chapter 6

- **Authenticity** | Children are not afraid to be themselves. Our obsession with excellence sometimes clouds the fact that worship can be playful and fun. Having children leading in a variety of roles injects the service with a level of authenticity that is contagious.

- **"Big People Respond to Little People"** | When children lead, adults tend to lean in—not out. In other words, as Dr. Melody Kuphal from Hosanna! Lutheran Church noted, "Big people respond to little people." There is something disarming, joyful, and deeply human about watching a child lead worship that invites even the most reserved adults to participate more fully.

Challenges

- **More Risk** | Things will inevitably go "wrong" when children are leading in worship, whether it's a missed cue or forgotten line. Yet, this imperfection is part of the beauty of children leading. The risk is worth taking, for in these moments, we witness the Kingdom of God at work.

- **More Time** | Including children meaningfully in worship—especially in planning—requires time, intentionality, and support structures. It's far more than handing them an instrument on Sunday. Adults at church and at home must be willing to listen, mentor, adapt, and sometimes slow down the process so that children's contributions are truly valued and understood.

- **Children Feeling Pressure from Adults** | Children may feel pressure—spoken or unspoken—to conform to adult expectations of "appropriate" worship behavior, which can stifle their creativity or authenticity. As Pastor Thomas noted at another point in our interview, children sometimes restrain themselves in worship because of how they perceive adult discomfort with expressive or liberated forms of praise.

- **Being "Cute" versus Being Faithful** | Even with regular involvement, there can be a lingering temptation for some congregants to see child-led elements as cute or entertaining rather than as spiritually formative. While this may likely go away with regularly programmed children's leadership, this mindset risks reinforcing a hierarchical view of worship participation and undercuts the theological claim that children are full participants in the body of Christ.

- **Audio Mixing** | Achieving a polished sound—whether in-house or online—requires significant intentionality and training, especially when children are involved. Children need guidance in microphone use and sound regulation, which can increase the demands on your audio engineers on Sundays. Amplification strategies that don't require children to hold a microphone can help reduce some of these challenges.

Next Steps

I recognize that for many reading this book, it may seem like an impossible task to get buy-in from your music ministers or your senior leaders. While it may sound like a silly starting point, encourage them to read the first few sections of this chapter—everything up to this point (you can even scan it for them—I won't tell the copyright police, I promise!). Speaking from experience, many leaders have not been challenged to incorporate children into worship, especially contemporary worship. It simply isn't part of the culture in most congregations. But that can be changed incrementally, and your leadership can help spark that change.

Begin by building bridges between children's ministry leaders and the leaders of your music and worship programming. Each congregation will be structured differently, but one thing remains constant: children's ministry leaders are often the people who know those children best. They can offer time-tested wisdom about how to work with specific kids and help communicate helpful strategies of empowerment to other leaders.

As with all changes, start small and plan for gradual growth. Not every child will start by reading Scripture aloud, singing in a choir, or playing an instrument with the worship band. Create a range of leadership opportunities—from passing out offering plates to designing artwork for bulletins—that allow for gradual engagement based on each child's gifts and comfort level.

Even when starting small, it helps to have a plan. While involving children every week may be a dream goal, it's not realistic for most churches. If you currently have no child involvement at all, aim to start quarterly, then move to monthly. You can build from there.

Regular scheduling is good for families, too. The reality is that we live in an overprogrammed world. Parents are making plans months in advance for their children, and calendars fill quickly. When you are able to think ahead and roster children for future leadership opportunities, it allows parents to help prepare them and attend any needed rehearsals.

Consider an apprenticeship model with children. For example, a 10-year-old could help lead worship through sound mixing or by advancing slides on ProPresenter, shadowing and leading alongside an adult who does this regularly. You'll want to remain mindful of your congregation's safety policies (typically requiring two non-related adults to be present at all times), but apprenticeship can be a powerful model for investing in children and providing hands-on training.

Finally, include children in the planning of worship. This is a great way to identify the songs and themes that resonate with them, and to make technical or programmatic adjustments that reflect their perspectives. If your meeting schedule or other constraints make that difficult, consider hosting occasional feedback sessions where children and families are intentionally invited to share their thoughts.

Don't Overthink This

As you make plans to better incorporate children into contemporary worship, do not overthink it. Children's ministry leaders and worship leaders alike value excellent vision and proper planning, but resist the urge to delay the incorporation of children until your plans are "perfect." There is no perfect or model way to make this happen—just start.

If the psalmist is correct that God inhabits the praises of God's people, then God is inhabiting those same praises when children lead us. The case studies in this chapter show that this kind of leadership is not only possible—it's already happening. And where it's happening, it's transforming congregations.

So, let the children lead in contemporary worship—not just because it's good for them, but because it's good for everyone. Let them remind us of what joy looks like. Let them interrupt our pursuit of flawless excellence with messy faithfulness. And in letting the children lead in contemporary worship services, we may find ourselves becoming more like the Kingdom we've been praying for all along.

Resources to Engage

Visit abingdonpress.com/children-lead-extras for additional information and links to the following resources.

Brentwood Benson
A music publishing company that features collections of contemporary worship songs for children's choirs or young worship leaders in band-led settings.

Nelson Cowan, editor. *Worship Any Time or Place: The Compact Book of Methodist Liturgies, Prayers, and Other Acts of Blessing.* Abingdon Press, 2024. Includes an intergenerational Great Thanksgiving (prayer for Holy Communion) that can be used in contemporary worship settings.

Chapter 6

The Gospel Story Hymnal, Word & Wonder
This hymnal includes over 150 well-known songs that are woven into a thoughtful retelling of the story of scripture, accompanied by bright illustrations and child-friendly notes on scriptural themes, theological concepts, and ideas for living out the faith.

"Amplifying Child Vocals In Productions." ProSoundWeb
An article that is technical in nature about best ways to capture the voices of children in live sound environments.

Doorpost Songs
Offering scripture-based resources—including song videos, sheet music, tracks, and curriculum—to raise up a new generation of worshipers.

Chapter 7

The Old Has Gone, the New Is Here

In 2 Corinthians 5, Paul boldly proclaims, "Therefore if anyone is in Christ, the new creation has come: The old has gone, the new is here!" He is speaking about the pivot point in our faith: when we are saved by the grace of Jesus Christ through faith, we are already a new creation. Yet even though we have *become* this new creation, our work isn't finished—we are also *becoming* more like Christ by the power of the Holy Spirit.

Paul's claim here also gestures to the wider scope of God's plan of salvation and where we find ourselves within it. We are between the Creation and the New Creation. We are between the First Coming of Christ in the Incarnation and his Second Coming in the consummation of all things. We are between the Church militant (the Church on earth) and the Church triumphant (the Church in heaven).

We are an in-between people, belonging to in-between institutions, following a go-between God.

But as we know from so many experiences, while "the old" passed away in principle, it sure still seems to linger. This can be especially true in local church life. I'm sure you have lost count of the number of times folks have been resistant to change or have unknowingly weaponized phrases like "we've never done it this way before." Sociologist Ann Swidler argues

Chapter 7

that these "old orders" are quite resilient—be it ideologies or other ways of thinking—and often hide themselves in the minutiae of everyday life.

When it comes to engaging children in worship, what are some of our hidden assumptions? How might they reflect a lingering and resilient "old order" in the rhythms of church life? And how might we respond?

Framed theologically, what are some "old orders" that could be limiting the Church's imagination when it comes to intergenerational worship? This chapter presents four theologically rooted and research-backed takeaways that challenge some well-meaning assumptions and offer "new" ways to think about children's participation. I put "new" in quotation marks because, as the writer of Ecclesiastes 1:9 aptly points out, "There's nothing new under the sun." Even so, what seems new may actually be something older that God is calling us to reclaim.

~~Be Serious~~ Be Playful

Seriousness in worship is an ecumenical phenomenon. When attending a traditional Mainline Protestant worship service, a level of formality may exude from the organ prelude, the acolytes who ceremoniously light the candles, the sitting, standing, or kneeling of the congregants at various points, the sincere but muted congregational response of "hear our prayer" in the intercessions. In a nondenominational or Evangelical church, worship may feel more serious as the house lights dim, as the midtempo songs convert to slower, more anthemic songs, as people get out their notebooks to fastidiously jot down notes and verbatim quotes from the pastor who speaks for 30-45 minutes, and as every head is bowed and every eye is closed during the altar call. In Catholic and Orthodox traditions, seriousness emerges through a deep reverence for mystery, most clearly expressed in the centrality of the Eucharist.

To be serious in worship is not a bad thing, but it is one of those "old orders" that can be quite resilient when trying to include children in intergenerational worship. Imagine a child uncontrollably giggling as the pastor recounts the Words of Institution ("On the night in which he was betrayed, he took bread . . ."), or two siblings getting into an argument during the prayers of the people, or a preschooler saying "potty words" while reciting the Apostles' Creed. If you cringed at any of these intentionally extreme scenarios—as I did—then you know that worship is at least, in part, a serious affair.

At the same time, our seriousness in worship shows up in covert ways regarding children—giving them only a small amount of agency, or trying to keep them busy instead of inviting their intentional participation, or how children never seem to be in the mind of preachers when writing their sermons, or how parents receive inhospitable glances when children make child-like noises.

As much as seriousness is important to worship, so too is play. While the Bible never explicitly directs us to worship the Lord *playfully*, the theme of play echoes throughout the scriptures. In Proverbs 8, personified Wisdom rejoices and delights in creation, playfully present at God's side. King David dances before God with all his might in 2 Samuel 6. In the eighth chapter of the prophet Zechariah's vision about the restoration of Jerusalem, he speaks of the city streets being filled with children playing. The parables of Jesus are playful forms of storytelling, some of which equate entering the Kingdom with being childlike. And even in a serious moment in John 8, Jesus stoops down and draws in the sand—quietly, and perhaps playfully—as the crowd demands a response to the woman caught in adultery.

The Bible gives us theological imagination for play, and the sciences help us see how deeply it shapes us. According to the National Institute for Play, research across neuroscience and behavioral science demonstrates that play builds more complex brains, contributes to greater social and emotional intelligence, and leads to a better outlook on life. A play-filled life has positive impacts on trust, flexibility, optimism, problem-solving, emotional regulation, perseverance, empathy, openness, and belonging—for children and adults alike. What if we were all a bit more playful when it comes to worship across generations?

What's beautiful is that worship already does these things. We think, we emote, we connect with others, we move our bodies—we just don't

Chapter 7

think of this as "play." Our perceptions of worship have been clouded by the old order of seriousness.

So, let's re-frame our perspective and recognize that play and seriousness are not mutually exclusive. True intergenerational worship is both *seriously playful* and *playfully serious*. Worship can be reverent and lighthearted, structured and spontaneous, formative and fun. If we are *serious* about empowering children to lead in worship—whether from up front or from their seats—then we need to offer worship services that playfully welcome their energy and creativity. We need liturgies that create space for exploration and wonder. We need preaching that speaks to all ages—not just the adults.

And we need congregation members to catch this vision—even just a glimpse—as we see Zechariah's prophetic hope spring to life: sanctuaries and streets filled with all generations, rejoicing in God's saving work.

~~Be Engaged~~ Be Bored

As important as play is, it can't be our only mode in life or in worship—nor should it be. In a world that idolizes constant engagement and stimulation, worship invites us to slow down and to be still.

However, when it comes to children in worship, we have this tendency to overprogram their entire Sunday morning. We have inherited an ideology that children must be constantly engaged. It does not matter if the children are participating in intergenerational worship or doing their own thing in an age-segmented space—we feel the need to keep them busy.

I wonder: What's underneath that?

Are we guided by educational instincts, wanting these children to learn as much as possible in a short amount of time? Are we guided by caregiving instincts, thinking that a laundry list of activities will keep children from being a distraction to themselves or to others? Are we guided by pastoral instincts, hoping that children associate "fun" with the Church and want to keep coming back? Are we guided by evangelistic instincts, dreaming that children will come to know the saving love of God in Jesus Christ?

These are all excellent instincts, but I think something else is going on.

Boredom. We worry that children might attend worship, or Sunday school, or another program, and get *bored*. Boredom has a negative connotation in today's world, and when participants in a program are bored, this is often seen as a failure.

The truth is that everyone gets bored, especially in church. Some are just more honest about admitting it than others. I can testify to this. I have endured plenty of boredom (and inspired it, too) through extended times of announcements, sermons that have gone down one-too-many rabbit holes, or songs where perhaps we don't need to repeat the bridge again.

Throughout Church history, worship has never been designed for constant stimulation. Think of the desert fathers and mothers in the rhythms of monastic prayer, or the moments of intentional silence and stillness in the liturgy. I'm certain that not every monk or well-meaning observer of silence was fully committed the entire time. The mind wanders. Thoughts shift. Sometimes we're fully in, and other times we're fully out. This is especially true of children. Boredom in church is natural, as long as it's not the chief state of being.

In other words, let the children be bored.

According to a research compilation of the Child Mind Institute, boredom can actually benefit children by creating the space for problem-solving, adaptability, and creativity. It also helps them build resilience for the moments in life that aren't instantly gratifying. Framed theologically, boredom gives children—and all of us—the opportunity to "be still." In the stillness, we may discover how God is calling us to *be* in the next moment.

In 1967, Charles Hummel wrote a small essay, *Tyranny of the Urgent*, that later became a cherished business classic and regularly quoted phrase by ministry leaders today. Hummel's key insight is this: the urgent is not always the same as the important—and, in fact, urgency often crowds out what matters most.

Chapter 7

In our churches, when we constantly give children things to do, I wonder if we are unwittingly stoking a false sense of urgency? What if our actions are teaching children and their caregivers to be afraid of restlessness or boredom? Instead, perhaps it is our job to give them permission to dwell. To sit and listen. To doodle while half-hearing the pastor's sermon. To fall asleep in a pew and wake up knowing they are in a safe and welcoming community. Of course, children are wired in diverse ways and do not experience boredom in the same way—so this invitation to boredom is not one-size-fits-all.

Boredom doesn't mean something is wrong. It can be a gift—an option we graciously give (in moderation, of course).

If we want to form children spiritually, we must resist the temptation to overfill their time. Children and families are already burdened by an overscheduled world. Perhaps one of the most radical acts of resistance to the "old order" of constant engagement is designing worship that imagines boredom as part of the process—not something to be programmed away.

In the gospels, we frequently read about a "crowd" that gathers around Jesus. We are not given much specificity about the crowd's composition, but it's reasonable to assume that families were present. When Jesus was speaking, I like to imagine some children running around and playing, some listening with attentive ears, some eating a snack, and other children either bored or taking a quick nap in the arms of their parent. The beauty of the incarnation is that Jesus meets us in our full humanity—boredom and all.

Surely, if Jesus had a problem with kids being bored, we probably would have read about him asking for their attention!

While boredom should not be the status quo of children in intergenerational worship, it presents an opportunity for God's story to come alive—if not in that moment, perhaps in the ensuing important moments for which the present boredom paves the way.

Let children lead, let them participate, and let them be bored. God can work with that.

~~Be Observers~~ Be Leaders

There is an old order that lingers in many church systems: the idea that children are meant to be observers in worship—especially intergenerational worship. The common thinking is that children regularly leading is not a viable option. It requires too much time or coordination. It's unpredictable. So instead, we give children the occasional opportunity, often selecting those who are reliable and non-disruptive. And while it will be a "powerful moment"—that moment is often more tailored to the gaze of adults.

I don't raise this to sound overly critical, but I have experienced this dynamic time and time again in pastoral leadership. I have even contributed to it, and I know what it feels like to not have "enough time" or energy to incorporate children into leadership.

At the same time, when I think back to my own story and early calling to serving the Church, it's because I was invested in as a young person. Most pastors and ministry leaders I know can name a moment—or a season—when their gifts were nurtured during childhood or adolescence. They were invited not just to observe, but to lead.

The Bible is full of young leaders. The boy Samuel heard God's voice and became a priest, prophet, and judge. Not long after this, the boy David—the youngest of the siblings—was chosen to battle Goliath. David was later anointed as king by Samuel, likely when he was just a teenager. The wisdom literature of the Hebrew Bible highlights young Esther, who used her position to speak up for her people for "such a time as this." And in the New Testament, we read of Mary, likely a young teenager, who said yes to God's call to bear Christ into the world. In all these scenarios, God called these young ones and empowered them to lead.

Leadership is not something to be taken for granted. Investing in children and young adults now will yield some powerful spiritual dividends in terms of leadership. The Fullerton Longitudinal Study (FLS) shines some research-backed light on this. The FLS is an ongoing psychological study initiated in 1979 with 130 infants and their families. In 2011, there was a fascinating report about leadership based on qualitative research with participants who were 29 years old in 2008. In this report, we learn that

Chapter 7

academic intrinsic motivation is a key predictor of leadership outcomes. This intrinsic motivation is defined as "enjoyment of school learning characterized by an orientation toward mastery, curiosity, persistence, and the learning of challenging, difficult, and novel tasks." In other words, when students enjoy learning for the sake of learning—and not other extrinsic motivators—they are more likely to enjoy leadership as adults.

How can we create an environment in our worship services and Christian education offerings that can facilitate the development of intrinsic motivation in children? What skills or activities can we nurture their mastery of? How can we encourage them to be curious, ask good questions, and explore ideas? How can we challenge them through novel tasks that require significant effort? This can happen through curriculum, but more likely it happens through intergenerational mentoring relationships.

Imagine a 7-year-old girl who loves singing and does it well. Of course, joining a children's choir will help hone her gift and passion. But what if a key mentor gave her an opportunity for a solo and encouraged her to take voice lessons leading up to it? Let's say this same leader joyously watched the child's performance, then sat down with her and her family to debrief and made plans for her next challenge. Perhaps it is this investment that will inspire a true love of singing and help cement a key part of her identity from a young age. As ministry leaders, are we poised to make those kinds of spiritual investments in our youngest disciples?

This may involve a rearrangement of how we view corporate worship. Chapter 6 spoke about our obsession with "excellence" in making worship services flow perfectly, instead encouraging "faithfulness." What if faithfulness means viewing worship less as a performance stage and more as a laboratory? What if children—and all of us—were given space to experiment, to fail, and to learn?

One of the programs I help direct does just this, but in the context of a week-long summer camp. At Animate, the flagship program of the Center for Worship and the Arts at Samford University, teenagers and their adult mentors are exposed to a variety of liturgical traditions and expressions through our worship services, given practical instruction in the arts through our toolbox classes, and challenged to grow spiritually in small groups. The week culminates in the Festival of Worship, where teenagers are empowered to design, plan, and lead a 15-minute service of worship to their peers.

During the summer of 2023, I co-led a team of researchers in gathering qualitative interview and focus group data about this Animate experience. We were interested in how young people experienced liturgical difference, as well as how they felt about leading their peers in worship. According to our data (a small sample of 35 students), we learned that many students felt safer experimenting and leading in the Animate environment compared to their home churches. This was often due to the perceived thoughts or judgments of adults in their own congregations. Put differently, young people are more hesitant to try things in their home churches because they believe older adults will not receive them well.

If that perception is true—even in part—it should give us pause. It suggests that the "old order" still holds sway in many of our congregations, where children and young adults are viewed primarily as observers. Let's not give that old order any more power than it already has. We know that young people *can* lead, so let's step up, release control, and create the necessary conditions to nurture their intrinsic motivations so that they *will* lead us—capably, skillfully, and faithfully.

~~Be Secondary~~ Be Primary

In 1529, Protestant reformer Martin Luther assembled the Small Catechism, which is a fascinating window into intergenerational Christian education. The catechism included texts and explanations of the Ten Commandments, the Apostles' Creed, the Lord's Prayer, and Luther's perspectives on baptism, confession, communion, daily prayer, and other duties of a Christian. Written in question-and-answer format, the "head of the household" was supposed to teach the children in a "simple way," encouraging them to learn the answers to these questions, internalizing core elements of the Protestant faith.

Luther and the other reformers were charting a new, but separate course from the Roman Catholic Church. Because of this, many Protestant

Chapter 7

sermons, writings, and approaches to catechesis and spiritual formation had a strong emphasis on didacticism. As the various Protestant reformations continued to spread, the bulk of that teaching was encouraged to take place in the home. As such, family-centered worship and instruction has been a hallmark of Protestantism for the last 450 years.

Since the second half of the twentieth century, the role of the family in religious education certainly has not disappeared, but it has become secondary. As denominations and local churches became increasingly professionalized in their leadership structures, the responsibility for children's spiritual formation shifted from the home to the local church. At the same time, church membership declined, and many parents—raised in a professionalized model themselves—began to feel unqualified to nurture faith at home. The result has been a perfect storm: parents increasingly look to the local church to form their children in the faith, while many churches struggle to meet expectations amid dwindling resources and attendance.

Unlike the first three situations in this chapter, I believe this "old order"—parents and caregivers as primary spiritual leaders—is worth recovering.

Research affirms this. The National Study of Youth and Religion (NSYR), led by Dr. Christian Smith of the University of Notre Dame, contains one of the largest data sets on intergenerational faith transmission. The biggest takeaway from this robust study? The most causal influence on the religious lives of American teenagers and young adults is the religious lives of their parents.

The implications of this are clear: if we want children to have a resilient, lasting faith, we are called to form *families*—not just children. Intergenerational worship on Sunday mornings is a good place to start, especially for parents or caregivers who may feel uncertain about their own religious literacy. The shared experience of liturgy, music, and proclamation can encourage the formation of all without embarrassment or stigma.

But what about Monday? As pastors and church leaders, how are we equipping families with practical tools to develop their faith from Monday through Saturday? Families need worshipful resources for the dinner table, the carpool line, morning and evening routines, sporting events, and even times of well-deserved vacation rest. Sure, they can search for these tools online, but the local church has an opportunity to step into this gap, identify the need, and resource families either with original content or by pointing them to trustworthy materials.

Recovering the old order of parents as primary spiritual leaders is not about nostalgia or tradition for its own sake. The religious landscape has changed—parents and children alike need support in their formation. When churches empower families to practice faith together, both on Sunday and throughout the week, we plant seeds that will bear fruit for generations to come.

Out with the Old, In with the New

Worship should be serious, but also playful. It should be engaging, but also leave room for boredom. It should let children observe, but empower them to lead more frequently. It should form families on Sunday—but even more so on Monday through Saturday.

These aren't quick tips. They are invitations to unmask these resilient old orders in our congregational life and to confront them with fresh vision. If it is indeed true that in Christ, the old has gone and the new is here, then newness abounds for our approaches to worship with children and families.

This kind of newness takes courage, creativity, and—thankfully—a childlike faith.

Conclusion
No Longer Strangers or Guests

As an academic, I love dwelling in theory, sitting with big thoughts and ideas, reflecting on them, then moving along to another book or journal article. Even as a teenager, I gravitated toward those kinds of books—long before I had the credentials to call myself an academic.

When I pastored churches, I would attend clergy meetings and hear about great leadership books my colleagues were reading. Sometimes I was gifted copies; other times, I bought them out of obligation. It's not because I didn't believe I needed to grow in my leadership. It's because of the pressure and burden I imposed upon myself when reading them. Leadership books and step-by-step books often left me feeling like I was perpetually behind.

The same feelings arose when I became a parent. In addition to the welcome—and not-so-welcome—advice from family members, there are so many experts out there with a seemingly unending amount of content. Moreover, these experts often do not agree with one another and even offer contradictory content! How do I wade through all of this as a parent? And why is this parenting stuff not as intuitive as it should be? More often than I care to admit, I have felt like I am not doing enough.

Perhaps this also resonates with you.

Conclusion

And perhaps you're wrestling with these feelings of insufficiency after reading this book. You're wondering if you are really doing enough to engage children in your pastoral ministry. Or you're overwhelmed by thinking about all the potential work ahead. Maybe you're a parent or caregiver, feeling the weight of guilt for what you haven't done in the present or the past.

Take heart. The fact that you've made it this far demonstrates that you care and are committed to growing. The good news is that God will shepherd us through this.

In 1719, hymnwriter Isaac Watts published the hymn "My Shepherd Will Supply My Need," which was an adaptation of Psalm 23. Just like the psalm, this hymn reminds us that God will meet our needs, give us a place to rest, and lead us to trust in God's sufficiency.

At the conclusion of the hymn, Watts took some liberties with scriptural interpretation. In the final stanzas, he writes:

> The sure provisions of my God
> Attend me all my days
> O may thy house be mine abode
> And all my work be praise
>
> There I would find a settled rest
> While others go and come
> No more a stranger or a guest
> But like a child at home

The original text of Psalm 23 in the King James Version concludes with: "and I will dwell in the house of the Lord forever," yet Watts beautifully reimagines our dwelling in this house as "settled rest" like "a child at home."

Watts' final image reminds us that God's dwelling place is like a home. Throughout this book, we've considered what it means for the Church to be not only a place of "settled rest" for children and families, but also an incubator of belonging and leadership. Each chapter has taken us one step further in imagining how this could be actualized in our churches.

We began with some theological unlearning and reframing, with resisting the "transactional model" of ministry as our starting point. As a reminder, a transactional model of ministry is when churches or ministries make intentional programmatic changes with the hoped-for outcome of increased attendance, participation, or commitment to the organization.

If that's our starting point for engaging children in intergenerational worship, then we need to reframe our convictions: from a focus on preserving the institution to advancing the Kingdom, from being obsessed with numerical economics to embracing the numerical blessing of children already in our midst, from spoon-feeding faith to respecting and developing agency, and from focusing on formation only on Sundays to embracing a full week of possibilities.

We then featured five different models of empowering children in worship, highlighting case studies of congregations, organizations, and leaders who are doing this work well.

The **first model** focused on creating hospitable space for children and families, as seen at Radiance Community Church and South Church, where pray-grounds—set-apart areas near the front of the sanctuary—invited intergenerational creativity and active participation in worship.

The **second model** addressed the inclusion of children with sensory sensitivities. Cross of Peace Lutheran Church and Eden Prairie United Methodist Church have made sensory awareness central to their worship planning, showing us what it means for all children to feel safe and welcome.

The **third model** emphasized intergenerational outreach-oriented worship. Through the global Messy Church movement and the performing arts ministry at Westover Hills United Methodist Church, we saw how worship can meet families where they are—especially outside the sanctuary walls—and become a bridge to the community.

The **fourth model** explored church-school partnerships. First United Methodist Church of Sarasota offered healthy, integrated practices between congregation and preschool, while Trinity United Methodist

Church in Colusa, California, through its *Sound Space* program, modeled the transformative potential of after-school music education.

The **fifth model** stressed the need for children's leadership in contemporary worship. At Hutchinson Missionary Baptist Church, monthly children-and-youth Sundays demonstrated the power of consistent inclusion, both in leading and planning. At Hosanna! Lutheran Church, we saw a musical pathway that begins in early childhood and continues into college, nurturing a generation of worship leaders with deep roots in their local church.

After these five models, I offered four theologically informed and research-backed takeaways, emphasizing the formative value of play, the surprising importance of boredom, the generational benefits of childhood leadership development, and the necessity of empowering parents and caregivers to be faith leaders in the home.

Perhaps something from one of these chapters inspired you. If so, don't give in to the temptation to rush right in and start *doing*. Sit with it. Reflect. Talk about these ideas in community—with pastors, leaders, parents, caregivers, and children themselves. Centering children and investing in their leadership does not happen overnight with a perfectly hatched programmatic plan. It involves faithful and prayerfully measured steps.

Worship-based models that are truly intergenerational can start small. Begin with the people and the resources already in front of you. Ask good questions. Experiment. Consult other churches who are doing this well. You are not alone in this.

And along the way, remember to check your intentions: children are not a transaction. They are not a tool for institutional growth, a problem to be solved, or an age-group delegated only to specialists. They are fellow worshipers—image-bearers, theologians, artists, questioners, playmates, and co-laborers in the life of the Church. When we make space for their leadership, we are receiving them as Christ would, and in doing so, Luke 9:48 teaches us that we welcome Christ himself.

This kind of welcome should shape the intergenerational spaces we create. May our congregations and programs become places where children are no longer strangers or guests, but in the words of Watts, like a child at home—comfortable, cared for, empowered.

I pray for the day when "all are welcome" equally applies to children.

I pray for the day when children leading in worship is no longer novel.

I pray for the day when intergenerational worship is not an experiment, but the norm.

I pray for the day when children are not just "the Church of the future," but the Church here and now.

That day could be sooner than we think, with your help.

Let the children lead.

www.ingramcontent.com/pod-product-compliance
Lightning Source LLC
Chambersburg PA
CBHW010048100426
42734CB00042B/3248